Learning *with* Learning Disability

This book uses the concept of "learning disability" to explore what it means to be human. It argues that we need to learn *with* rather than *from* or *about* learning disability. This crucial distinction means being open to what learning disability can teach us about what it means to be human. This approach comes from recognising learning disability as an organising concept – a concept which radically transforms our sense of what it means to be – or not be – a person.

After reflecting on the author's relationship to learning disability, the book explores relationships and tensions between conceptualisations of learning disability and of the human. Through historical ontology, the book initially examines how the phenomenon of "learning disability" came into being. It then explores ways in which the concept of learning disability has, over the course of the 20th and 21st centuries, radically transformed our sense not only of education and learning, but also of who is or is not deemed entitled to full citizenship and the associated rights, and so who is or is not fully human.

Each chapter of the book exposes tensions and contradictions apparent in the ways we tend to think about personhood and learning disability, illuminating them through a series a binary oppositions: human *and* not fully human; menacing *and* vulnerable; controlled *and* abandoned; capable *and* incapable; human *and* posthuman.

The book concludes by drawing together these tensions and contradictions to challenge the prevailing metanarrative of disability and make the case for a more inclusive conceptualisation of what it means to be human.

It will be of interest to all scholars and students of disability studies, the history of learning disability, humanism and posthumanism, and learning disability advocacy.

Owen Barden is Assistant Professor in Intellectual Disability and Inclusion at Trinity College Dublin, Ireland. He has published extensively on learning disability, with particular interests in histories of learning disabilities and participatory methodologies.

Autocritical Disability Studies

Series Editor: David Bolt
Liverpool Hope University, UK

This new book series represents both a contribution to, and a departure from, the academic field of critical disability studies. According to some concerns about that field, disability is the start but never the finish, there is insufficient engagement with the ethical and political issues faced by disabled people, and the work is too insensitive to individual experiences. Such concerns are addressed boldly in the new series via a formal coupling of critical disability studies with the research method of autoethnography.

The qualitative method of autoethnography acknowledges a researcher's individual experience in the most explicit of ways, from the very start of the process to the finished product that reaches publication. Whereas most traditional research methods claim, or at least aspire to, objectivity, autoethnography owns its subjectivity as paramount. This being so, when academic authors/editors have direct or at least intimate individual experience of disability, the subjectivity of their books can predicate a shift in typology from critical disability studies to what the new series terms autocritical disability studies.

In encouraging textual and theoretical work, the series also introduces autocritical discourse analysis and autocritical disability theory to formalise the ethical and epistemological importance of disability experience in many aspects of critical studies. The key point about the books sought for the series, then, is precisely that the individual experience of disability is recognised and positioned as both start and finish.

The book series editor, Professor David Bolt, encourages expressions of interest from potential monograph authors and volume editors.

Learning *with* Learning Disability
What Learning Disability Can Teach Us About Being Human
Owen Barden

For a full list of titles in this series, please visit: https://www.routledge.com/Autocritical-Disability-Studies/book-series/ASHSERADS

Learning *with* Learning Disability

What Learning Disability Can Teach Us About Being Human

Owen Barden

Routledge
Taylor & Francis Group
LONDON AND NEW YORK

First published 2026
by Routledge
4 Park Square, Milton Park, Abingdon, Oxon OX14 4RN

and by Routledge
605 Third Avenue, New York, NY 10158

Routledge is an imprint of the Taylor & Francis Group, an informa business

British Library Cataloguing-in-Publication Data
A catalogue record for this book is available from the British Library

ISBN: 978-1-032-53413-8 (hbk)
ISBN: 978-1-032-53414-5 (pbk)
ISBN: 978-1-003-41192-5 (ebk)

DOI: 10.4324/9781003411925

Typeset in Sabon
by Apex CoVantage, LLC

This book is dedicated to Lucy, Holly and Freddie B.

Contents

Figures

Acknowledgements

I owe an enormous debt of gratitude to my colleague, mentor and friend David Bolt. Not just for persuading me to write this book, but for all the support, encouragement and opportunities he has given me over the years. Thank you, David.

I would also like to acknowledge Claire Penketh and all my former colleagues at the Centre for Culture and Disability Studies and Liverpool Hope University. Much love to you all.

Thanks also to my co-researchers and colleagues at The Brain Charity in Liverpool and TRAC at the University of Wales, especially Steve Walden, Stacey Rees, Rhiannon Currie and Samantha Taylor.

I must also thank Liz Tilley and Nathaniel Lawford at The Open University and my colleagues at The University of Iceland, especially Sola Ólafsdóttir and Guðrún Valgerður Stefánsdóttir for permission to share our work on emotional communities in Chapter 5.

Finally, thanks to many colleagues at Trinity College Dublin, and particularly the Trinity Centre for People with Intellectual Disabilities, who have made me so welcome upon my recent arrival. Especial thanks to Michael Shevlin for your thoughts on Chapter 6.

Preface

This is a book about learning disability. It is a kind of history of learning disability: a history of the concept of what we now call learning disability, at least in the UK. This concept goes by other names in other places – for example, intellectual disability in the United States and Australasia. There have been many such labels over time, and no doubt new ones will appear. Disability terminology is always freighted and fraught; there is no word or set of phrases that pleases everyone. I have taken the liberty of being quite flexible, choosing the word or phrase that seemed most appropriate for the context. Sometimes this is *people with learning disabilities*, sometimes *learning-disabled people*, and sometimes historical and pejorative terms like *moron* that might jar contemporary sensibilities. The idea is not to shock or offend but also not to shy away from confronting these problematic terms.

Our vacillations over what to call this particular "thing" point as much to our wariness of learning disability (or whatever you want to call it) as to any advances in our understanding of it. This book does not seek to offer a new label, but it does seek to offer something to our understanding of learning disability. The central argument is that learning disability has much to teach us about what it means to be human. I draw on evidence not just from disability studies and learning disability discourse, but also from educational, moral and disability philosophy as well as cognitive psychology and the medical humanities to show how our understanding of what it means to be human is heavily dependent on our conceptualisations of what we currently call learning disability. So, this is also a book about the history of intelligence and about how our understanding of personhood has changed over the last 200 years or so.

I introduce the book as an autocritical history of learning disability. Although much has been written on the history of learning disability, I believe this book may be the first autocritical history. As such, it makes methodological contribution that may be of interest to historians as well as scholars working in those disciplines named above. What I mean by an autocritical history of learning disability is a history that is reflexive in its attention to my positionality as a highly privileged, non-disabled scholar. Rather than objectify people labelled with learning disabilities, as so much research has done, the aims are firstly to objectify my own subjectivity and then to objectify the concept of learning disability itself, in order to bring it under critical scrutiny. This critical scrutiny forms the bulk of the book. The history of learning disability is often an uncomfortable, even distressing one – and the importance of emotions in such research is also discussed – but the book finishes optimistically. We can make the world a better place for everyone, if we choose to.

1 Introduction

An Autocritical History of Learning Disability

This chapter begins the book by positioning it within autocritical Disability Studies, as what might be termed an autocritical history of learning disability. This means that the book sits within critical Disability Studies and has an autoethnographic slant, most explicitly within this opening chapter, where I – a non-disabled academic – discuss my relationships with disability in general and learning disability specifically. I start by acknowledging two things. One, that the voices and knowledges of learning-disabled people have all too often been subjugated and silenced in both scholarly discourse and wider society. Two, that "Maybe there is nothing more ableist in character than a sole academic 'banging on' about the world" (Goodley, 2014: x). Simon Jarret and Liz Tilley, in their article on the history of the history of learning disability, make a similar point in drawing attention to Simone Aspis'[1] critique of researchers who use people with learning disabilities as "subjects to be examined and picked around" (Jarrett and Tilley, 2022: 2) in order to test non-disabled academics' hypotheses and make dubious claims of empowerment.

Against this backdrop, the chapter addresses the fundamental question of what right, if any, I have to write this book. In developing an answer, I will contend that in the study of learning disability, different people with different backgrounds, knowledges and expertise can make different, equally valuable contributions to the discourse, and generate diverse outputs and impacts – and that this is a good thing. This argument applies Rosemarie Garland-Thomson's contention that disability is a generative resource, one which benefits society (Garland-Thomson, 2015), to the study of learning disability. The idea is that through examining critically and honestly tensions and contradictions in our assumptions about learning disability and about personhood that we can collectively reach a more inclusive understanding not just of learning disability, but what it means to be human.

DOI: 10.4324/9781003411925-1

This first chapter is the hardest to write. If the mantra of disability rights, and Disability Studies, is "nothing about us without us", then what right does a lone, non-disabled academic write a book about learning disability? A book which has no direct input from anyone with a learning disability cannot claim the authenticity of lived experience, nor the emancipatory agency of participatory research? How do I avoid becoming one of the "tarmac professors" the late Mike Oliver railed against, rolling over disabled people in order only to advance my own career (Oliver, 2002)? And how do I write about my own relationship with disability and learning disability with being self-indulgent? Self-serving and self-justifying? Patronising? Boring? Moreover, how do I write about learning disability at length without reifying it as a "thing" – an object which undoubtedly exists, when all we really know for sure that it is merely a historically contingent idea, an unstable changeling, a shifting cultural construct (Goodey, 2011)? I'm not sure that I can, but to try and address these questions, I make the case that learning disability is an integral part of being human, and therefore part of us and of the world we live in. I am not suggesting that we are all disabled somehow, even though it may be true that – to quote another mantra – we all become disabled if we live long enough. Rather, inspired by Tim Ingold's (Ingold, 2018) theorising of anthropology and of education, I make the case for learning *with* rather than *from* learning disability. What does this mean? It means I am trying to avoid trite suggestions that non-disabled people have much they could learn from learning-disabled people. It means that learning disability, in whatever terminological guise, has at its core much to tell us about being human. It means using the concept of learning disability as a tool for thinking: thinking about culture, about disability, and above all, what it means to be human. After all, disability might be the start of our investigations, but it is never the finish (Goodley, 2014).

Going to School with Learning Disability

This book is therefore essentially a project in which I attempt to come to know what learning disability is, and what it can teach us about being human. In a way, this is *going to school with learning disability*, which is a way of saying that the book is about *educating myself about* learning disability by *corresponding with* it. In *Anthropology and/as Education*, which has had a very significant influence on my thinking for this book, Tim Ingold writes beautifully about education as a means of attending to the world, of bringing us into correspondence with the world. Research – like that required to write a book like this – is, of course, one way in which we educate ourselves. Research is typically defined as some form of systematic, critical, reflective inquiry which seeks to contribute to the sum of knowledge. Education, meanwhile, can be defined as process involving activities that bring about learning that is valued, worthwhile and that contributes to the development of the person, with the intervention of a teacher (Pring, 2000). So, although research can be a form of education through which we teach ourselves, more commonly the teacher is someone or something else. Etymologically, education means "to lead out", whilst attend means "stretch towards" (Latin – *ad* – toward; *tendere* – stretch). And to correspond means to co-respond – to answer to one another and go along together.

Ingold's is not a book about disability, nor is it written from a Disability Studies perspective, and so it is all the more intriguing – and encouraging – that he illustrates his idea of education happening through co-respondence with productive uncertainties by drawing on the work of Erin Manning. Manning wrote about her experiences of the world through what she termed "autistic perception" in *The Minor Gesture* (Manning, 2016). In contrast to Ingold's work, *The Minor Gesture* can, I think, be reasonably considered as belonging to Disability Studies, and critical autism studies in particular. Ingold acknowledges the difficulties around non-disabled people attempting to adopt or mimic a disabled person's perspective, and of disability simulation, and wonders about the possibility and potential of taking the experience of autism – which for Manning includes full attention to matters of interest, complexity of experience, and lingering in uncertainty – as the starting point for inquiry, rather than – as the psychomedical professions and many philosophers might have it – an abnormality, or as a condition to grow out of or supersede with reason. Could we, Ingold asks, rather than trying to override or eradicate this mode of attention to the world, instead co-respond and communicate with it, and hence learn from it? Not, as non-autistics, claim to be "a bit autistic" nor to inhabit a simulacrum of autism, but to be enlivened by it, to stretch towards it whilst recognising that it can never be fully and finally defined or categorised. I would like to expand this attempt beyond autism to learning disability more generally.[2] To, as Ingold would have it, "set aside the armour of received explications and understandings and form a habit of attending to and caring for" learning disability (2018: 40).

And so my intention with this book is to attend to and correspond with learning disability, to stretch reflexively towards it, and to keep it present in our considerations of what it means to be human, so that we can all – learning disabled and not – go along better together. This is what it means to learn *with* – not from or about – learning disability. "With-ness", says Ingold, "saves the other from objectification by bringing it alongside as a companion or accomplice. It turns othering into togethering" (2018: 26). With-ness recognises that there can be no meaningful communication unless "there is variation in what each participant brings" to the sharing of experience, and the sharing of experience is what I am here calling "school". The argument is not that we are all the same because we share a common humanity, but that we are all different, and that it is through that continual creation of difference that we can educate ourselves about the meanings of both learning disability and what it means to be human. Each of us has our gifts to give, and this notion is embedded in the Latin etymology of community. The *com* means "together", and *munus* means "gift", as in *munificence*. Although I admire the spirit of Ingold's claim, I don't pretend to avoid objectification completely, and I am not sure it's even possible. I do strive to avoid the objectification of learning-disabled people, and instead bring myself, the concept learning disability, and relationships between the two under some kind of objective scrutiny.

There is thus an ontological dimension to this work, since I'll be trying to understand the very nature of learning disability and of personhood. In studying learning disability in order to try and come to an understanding of it – and hence personhood – I will treat it not as a mere object but as an animate *thing* in its own right, with which I am trying to correspond. There are many ways in which the animated existence of learning disability is evident. Perhaps the most obvious is the ever-changing terminology used in relation to "the thing" and people said to have "the thing" (Trent, 1994: 6) now known as learning disability (or intellectual disability, or cognitive impairment, or whatever). Even before early professional medical diagnoses like "idiot" and "imbecile", people who might now be labelled with learning disabilities were referred to superstitiously changelings or shapeshifters (Berger, 2014), but it would be more accurate to regard learning disability itself as the shapeshifter, given its perpetually evolving contours and labels.

Another way in which learning disability's animate role in society is evident is through the philosophical, political and economic work that it does (McDermott *et al.*, 2006). This work is manifold. Throughout the 19th and 20th centuries and on into the 21st century, learning disability has, philosophically and empirically, provided Others against which Normals can be measured; it has legitimated professional medical, legal, educational and health power-knowledge regimes; it has been prominent in powerful intersecting discourses, including those of medicine, education, media, law, economics, politics, philosophy, colonialism and eugenics; it has provided careers for professionals and care for fellow humans labelled as defective, simultaneously casting professionals as moral agents working for the good of society and people labelled with learning disabilities and its synonyms as immoral or amoral agents (Barden, 2020b).

In addition to all this, learning disability has, in its numerous guises, figured large in aesthetic discourse and our cultural imagination and texts. James Berger (Berger, 2014), Patrick McDonagh (McDonagh, 2008) and Michael Bérubé (Bérubé, 2016), for example, all have written extensively about the importance of learning disability in fiction. While Bérubé focuses on how an understanding of learning disability transforms our understanding of narrative, and McDonagh traces a history back to William Wordsworth's *The Idiot Boy*, Berger makes the argument that the ubiquity of what he calls the cognitively impaired and "disarticulate", including their presence in canonical modernist texts like William Faulkner's *The Sound and the Fury* and Joseph Conrad's *The Secret Agent*, makes them central to making sense of humanity and culture. He goes on to make the claim, perhaps a counter-intuitive one, that the emotional investment evident in the creation and consumption of these characters means that writers and perhaps readers – therefore *desire* learning disability, foreshadowing more recent work on what it might mean to desire disability (Goodley *et al.*, 2021). Incidentally, Berger's term *disarticulate* has a useful double meaning: in one sense, it denotes those who do not articulate – speak – in normative ways. Simultaneously, it denotes those people who are separated, or more literally *disjointed* from the main body of society. It is another way of acknowledging the perpetual outgroup status of learning-disabled people, even as they are crucial to our conceptions of humanity and society (Goodey, 2016).

Now, by definition, treating something as a "thing" involves objectification, and this is somewhere where considerable care is needed. The scientific and educational study of learning disability has been formed through objectification of learning-disabled people. Scientists and pedagogues stand outside learning disability and yet somehow are the ones deemed to have the knowledge to explain it. People labelled with learning disabilities have knowledge of learning disability and yet historically their perspectives have tended to be ignored, partly because they are deemed incapable of rational thought. As Ingold puts it, in his critique of scientific knowledge:

> On one side of binary are scientists and other people *of* Culture; on the other side are the custodians of traditional knowledge, people *in* culture. And if the latter, not knowing what they know, are to cross the Rubicon from tradition to reason, then paradoxically, they need science to re-educate them in their own knowledge, to explain it back to them in formal terms, so that they can see how it might be used as an instrument of rational management and in order to free them from the shackles of the past.
>
> (2018: 14)

Critique of this binary division of knowers and known can be traced back to Jacque Ranciere, the 19th-century French philosopher who, in

The Ignorant Schoolmaster – published in 1818 – denounced what he called the myth of pedagogy, which relied on a parable of "knowing minds and ignorant ones, ripe minds and immature ones, the capable and the incapable, the intelligent and the stupid" (Rancière, 1991: 6). The division, which rests in large part on a distinction between those deemed able to reason (scientists and educators, for example) and those deemed not (children, indigenous peoples and people labelled with learning disabilities, for instance), persists to this day. We'll come on to consider the limits of rationality in relation to the problems of learning disability and modernity in Chapter 5, and for the moment stick to the issue of objectification. Firstly, the intention here is not to objectify learning-disabled people, but the "thing" currently known as learning disability. Secondly, the intention is not to try and transmit knowledge of learning disability back to learning-disabled people – even if such a thing were desirable, a book like this would not be a good place to attempt it. Instead, the intention is to use the concept of learning disability as tool for thinking about what it means to be human. In doing so, later chapters will draw on the voices of both scientists and people with learning disabilities. The desire to communicate and correspond with learning disability entails reflexivity, and reflexivity requires consideration of how one stands in relation to things. In other words, a phenomenological commitment to both acknowledging my own position in relation to learning disability and to confronting quizzically what it is and what it might be, whilst conceding that I can never know it perfectly, not only because it presents many faces but because of my own inescapable limitations. Yet it is such aporia that present the most fruitful territory for inquiry (Peim, 2018).

Nick Peim writes as a philosopher of education about this inescapable phenomenological dimension of research, and the necessity for researchers to reflect on how they position themselves in relation to the things they study. This he calls "objectifying the subjective":

> One significant point of beginning is represented in the experience of the researcher, not as a touch-feely, sentimental or confessional mode of engagement; but as a necessary prelude to locating the focus of the study in its proper context and in its inescapable relations with a given point or consciousness. The element of addressing one's own subjectivity I sometimes refer to as objectification of the subjective.
>
> (Peim, 2018: 19)

Peim sees this as a step not only towards contextualising an inquiry, but also towards understanding oneself and one's relationships with the world, guaranteeing originality in one's work and breaking down the false dichotomy of objective/subjective. To my mind, this follows from *The Problems of Philosophy*, in which Bertrand Russell showed, through thought experiments he undertook on the simple wooden desk he wrote on, how it is only the subjective that can ever truly be known (Russell, 1989). A desk might objectively be said to be rectangular in shape and brown in colour, but it rarely if ever appears as such to the person sitting at it: its shape and colour will inevitably vary according to the angle it is viewed from and the light it is viewed under. All we can ever truly know about are our subjective experiences of the desk, which will not correspond faithfully with objective facts about the desk, because it will rarely if ever appear to be simply rectangular and brown. It will appear to have some kind of diamond or parallelogram shape and to be multicoloured.

Yet subjects need objects to know about. And those objects only emerge through our perception of them. Subjects and objects are thus intertwined (Titchkosky, 2024). This is as true for learning disability as it is for desks. In a similar vein, it is possible to borrow another argument from Tim Ingold, itself derived from John Dewey, and *Experience and Education* in particular. This argument goes that traits – those supposedly objective characteristics of people – whether biological or cultural (and learning disability has been framed as both) are fallacious: the idea of genealogical traits is contradictory because habits and dispositions only emerge through experience in an environment, and not in isolation. This is another way of saying that you cannot be "born with" a learning disability; not only because such traits only arise within human culture, but also because the characteristics that comprise the trait are historically contingent and highly mutable. Learning disability has gathered some meanings over time just as it has shed others, through shared activities such as research, education, advocacy and support – and these meanings may be further modified by communicating with it. Understanding how and why these meanings have evolved over time, and may continue to do so in the future, is an aim of this book.

Objectifying my subjectivity is also a way of acknowledging my role as a gatekeeper of knowledge, and my epistemological ignorance (Carlson, 2010) – those things about learning disability I, as a non-disabled subject, can never truly know. This is the aporia I attempt to embrace in this book. I have to recognise that I am an academic working in a university. This is one kind of social institution which, through its power and protocols, claims to determine what counts as knowledge. And I am bound not only by my relationship to the institution and its policies and procedures, but by the conventions of genre; in this case the, academic book. The rules of genre determine not only the format in which knowledge is presented, but also to how I present myself. Normally, that would mean maintain the pretence of the scientific, disinterested, dispassionate observer – a character who is, of course, a mythical being. Yet these are not the only influences. I am putting forward my own perspectives and arguments, and they have been shaped by the world; both my personal experiences within it and the institutions and discourses relevant to my research. And so it is necessary to articulate who I am in relation to learning disability. I hope that my doing so does not come across as self-indulgent, nor reinforces the very relations that would usually set me apart from learning disability and learning-disabled people; people who, by and large, do not work in universities or read academic books (although it must be stressed that some do). As such, subsequent sections of this chapter offer brief autobiographical accounts of my relationships with disability generally, and then learning disability specifically. As a prelude to this short autobiography, and as a way of further deconstructing the objective/subjective binary, I want to first consider some things about learning disability and also the nature of research itself.

Caring about Learning Disability; Caring about Research

> Research is like finding pieces of the jigsaw. . . . It's looking over and over again. Because sometimes if you look at something once you don't get to see the full picture but when you come back and look at it again you'll see something different. And the more times you go backward and forward to it, the more you see. So that's good.
>
> (Cook and Inglis, 2009: 60)

This definition comes from an article published by Tina Cook and Pam Inglis, two highly regarded researchers of learning disability. They are well-known for using participatory methods with co-researchers who have been labelled with learning disabilities. But these are not their words. The quote comes from co-researcher on one of their research projects. In fact, from a man with a learning disability who was in a secure unit in a hospital at the time. I like it and include it here because it encapsulates the nature of the research endeavour concisely as well as any definition in a methodological textbook. It captures two aspects of the nature of research particularly well. Firstly, its iterative nature: the need to move back and forth across the object under investigation – or construction – until you see something different. Secondly, the need to stand back from the object in order to see the full picture. We might conceive of this picture, the full picture, as representing some kind of truth about the object of interest and its place in the world. And, of course, another way to define research is as a search for truth. However, the search for truth is not to be confused with objectivity. Rather, what we regard as truth reflects our participation in the world (Ingold, 2018).

As Nick Peim has argued, our knowledge and our quest for more of it cannot be detached from all the background knowledge, understanding, ways of seeing and sense of purpose that we bring, consciously or subconsciously, to bear on our investigation. We research things because we care about them, and such care arises from a kind of attachment to the objects we investigate, and entails a commitment which reveals something essential about how we conduct our everyday lives in relation to the world at large, and not just the objects we study. "Care" in its various guises will be a recurring motif in this book: caring about; caring for; care homes; care in the community; and capacity to care are some such guises relevant to learning disability.

Disability is often described as tragedy or misfortune, and sometimes – perhaps euphemistically – as a challenge. It is less commonly described as a blessing. However, Wolff (Wolff, 2010) makes the argument that disability can be conceived of as both a theoretical and a practical blessing, saying that if we confront and think through the issues it presents, it can lead us towards a more compassionate society. Is learning disability a blessing? Whilst it may not be something that people would tend to wish for (Sparrow, 2015), as a concept and characterisation it is certainly what might be called "a real problem" (Ingold, 2018) or "useful trouble" (Peim, 2018), and so a blessing in that sense. Real problems have no solutions, but they afford openings – opportunities – to see things anew. They must be given time for *patient experimentation*, which means opening a path and seeing where it takes you. A journey must be undertaken: intuitive, prospective, improvisational, speculative.

Similarly, things which are useful trouble encourage us to think through the distinction between how we perceive a thing and the nature of the thing itself. This means acknowledging – even objectifying – our own subjectivity whilst simultaneously studying the thing – learning disability, in my case – as an animate thing in its own right. A shifting, historically contingent, multifaceted construct. This is how learning disability becomes real – not just thinking about, or learning from it, but learning with it. Interestingly, even the first self-appointed experts on what we now call learning disability recognised this need to stand back from the object under investigation in order to try and appreciate and take account of its complexities. In 1861, the prominent physician P. Martin Duncan, a contemporary of John Langdon Down, whom Down's Syndrome is named after, decried the "paucity of reliable and trustworthy information on idiocy", the "hasty generalisations" and "baseless assertions" and stated that "the first steps of the truthful enquirer, when brought into contact with the objects of his study, are retrogressive. To unlearn is to take a great step in this" (Duncan and Millard, 1866: 233). This brings to mind the contemporary appeal from the eminent psychiatrist, neuroscientist and philosopher Iain McGilchrist for more empathetic and holistic thinking to cultivate more harmonious ways of being and help solve the problems the dominant techno-rationalist mode of thought in the West has wrought (McGilchrist, 2012). This is an issue we return to in Chapter 5, when we consider the relevance of posthuman philosophy to learning disability.

Despite – or perhaps because of – all the different definitions, paradigms and perspectives brought to bear upon it, the true nature of learning disability cannot be known in advance of this enquiry. And so the purpose of this book is thus to carefully explore, construct and elaborate some kind of truth about learning disability. This is not truth in the sense of supposedly objective – but actually manufactured – facts or empirical evidence (Packer, 2017). Such an approach would rest on a scientific approach which is incapable of adequately addressing the problems of modernity, many of which it has itself created. Nowhere is this more evident than in the ongoing exclusion, abuse and attempted extermination of people with learning disabilities. Neither is it truth in the sense of authentic lived experience of learning disability, for I have no such experience. Rather, it is a truth which reflects my participation in the world, a world which contains learning disability. It is a truth derived from confronting learning disability quizzically, thinking about what it is and what it might be, and which entails a deep ethical commitment.

The current times of crisis – using the word not in its contemporary sense of catastrophe but in its original Ancient Greek sense of turning point – afford opportunities to reframe how we think about learning disability, the people who acquire that label, and humanity, since "how we determine the nature of things determines the nature of the world" (Peim, 2018: xx). The first step in constructing this truth is to acknowledge unknown knowns – the beliefs, orientations and discourses that have produced me; to recognise that I am caught up in and care about learning disability, or more accurately the people who acquire that label, and that this shapes my argument. It means recognising my desire to attend to – reach out towards – learning disability in order to think about how learning disability and humanity might go along together better. It is about trying to do the right thing by learning *with* learning disability rather than *from* or *about* learning disability. In this sense, I want to *communicate with* learning disability; it is part of the environment and is of concern to me, and – because it is an aspect of human culture – to all of us. It arouses my – our – curiosity and so I am moved to respond. Both Peim and Ingold write compellingly about the way we research things that we care about, have an attachment to. This care is a kind of commitment to the things we investigate, things we are caught up with in our everyday relations with the world. These things can present us with real problems and useful trouble: issues that have no conclusive solutions, but afford opportunities to see things anew.

Learning disability is a real problem, it is useful trouble, because it can help us understand our relationships with each other, personhood and the world.

My Relationships with Disability and Learning Disability

Disability Studies scholars have repeatedly called for researchers to make explicit their relationships with disability. Over ten years ago, Joan Corbett O'Toole (O'Toole, 2013) argued that we need to talk about our relationships with disability, because those relationships lead to valuable differences in experiences of disability and ableism, and hence opportunities for reciprocal learning, for alliances, and for further theorising. She goes on to argue that *not* disclosing our relationships shuts down such opportunities, especially when "the signifier 'nondisabled' is always associated with able-bodied privilege" (np). Non-disclosure perpetuates the culturally embedded ableist idea that being non-disabled is the preferable way to be, and thus contradicts the affirmative tenets of the Disability Studies. Simi Linton makes a similar point:

> I think that it is incumbent on non-disabled scholars to pay particular attention to issues of their own identity, their own privilege as non-disabled people, and the relationship of these factors to their scholarship. . . . Stating one' s position relative to the subject matter is of theoretical importance and it is also of political importance. Stating that one identifies as disabled or nondisabled calls attention to the absent voice of disabled people in scholarship and illustrates that the reader may tend to make the assumption, although probably not consciously, that the writer is non-disabled. . . . I am suggesting that non-disabled and disabled scholars working in Disability Studies . . . discuss their subject position, and the consequences for their scholarship in similarly complex and meaningful ways.
>
> (Linton, 1998: 537)

I am non-disabled Disability Studies scholar. For better or worse, I am a white, middle-class, middle-aged, British non-disabled Disability Studies scholar. But I do have relationships with disability and impairment. One of my children is autistic. One of my parents has been living with cancer and neuropathy for many years. One of my parents has experienced mental health issues in various ways for much of their life, including a spell in an institution in their early 20s. One of my partner's parents experiences dementia, which is progressing rather rapidly. My sister gets around on a combination of crutches and an electric wheelchair. And I work in a University department with colleagues both disabled and not. I convene and teach a course there specifically for people with learning disabilities. In the grand scheme of things, not many people work in a department or teach a course like mine, but I don't think my experiences or relationships are that unusual; many if not most of us will have family members, friends and colleagues who are disabled. I would like to illustrate this point in two ways. The first is with a cartoon (Figure 1.1). This cartoon sits in a frame on my desk. It was given to me by my mother after I gained my doctorate in 2011. It is a signed original by the artist

Figure 1.1 Remember that you're unique, just like everyone else.

Simon Drew (and I love a bit of nominative determinism). The image is of a huddle[3] of penguins. I'm no ornithologist, but I think probably Emperor penguins. Anyway, being all the same species, the penguins all look similar to each other, but are not identical. And to emphasise this point, each is balancing a tennis ball on its head or beak. Close inspection reveals that each is balancing the ball in a slightly different way: the tip of the beak or the crown of the head, for instance. At the bottom of the image is a caption, which reads "remember that you're unique, just like everyone else".[4] The second way in which I would like to illustrate this point is with another phrase. The phrase is "same same but different". My sister, who I mentioned above, has lived in Cambodia for the last 14 years, and in Laos before that. I have been fortunate enough to visit her a few times. *Same same but different* is a phrase that originated in Thailand and can now be heard quite commonly there and South East Asia more widely. It means very similar, but a bit different. To me, both the penguin cartoon and *same same but different* encapsulate the idea that whilst we all have our unique set of relationships with disability and disabled people, there are also commonalities and similarities. And this brings us back to the centrality of disability to human lives and experiences.

But Joan Corbett O'Toole was right: until I wrote this – and said it at the biannual Disability & Disciplines conference at Liverpool Hope University in July 2023, where I worked at the time – my colleagues did not know anything about my familial relationships with people with impairments, even though I had worked with them for over a decade. They didn't ask, and I didn't tell. Were they worried about making me uncomfortable? Maybe. Did I have imposter syndrome? Definitely. But through stating my relationship to disability, I am hoping that as a non-disabled Disability Studies scholar, I can make a positive contribution to disability discourse and theory, and can be an ally for disabled people in the greater project of emancipation.

I came to care about learning disability specifically serendipitously. My caring is all the more conspicuous for that; for the first 20-odd years of my life, it was not something I gave much thought, and certainly not something I would have considered as contributing to my self-image (Jaworska, 2010). I don't have any lived experience of learning disability. In fact, as noted above, I embody many if not all of the personal characteristics that generate privilege. What contact do I have with people living with labels of learning disability? I mentioned that I have one autistic child. Although autism is commonly defined and referred to as a learning disability, my child does not see themselves as learning disabled. Academically, they do very well – for example, winning an engineering scholarship to help support their A-Level studies, and then going onto study biomedical engineering at university, specialising in prosthetics (further evidence of the way disability threads itself through our lives). My child finds some social and emotional things tricky but has a good circle of close friends, a weekend job which involves a lot of interaction with the public and is beginning to go to festivals and big concerts, driving themselves and their friends. They spent much of last year backpacking around the world. So it is difficult to characterise my child as having a learning disability, despite what the diagnostic manuals, codes of practice and charity websites say. It might also be possible to attempt to make a case that my latter-day experiences with parental dementia might give some insight into learning disability, since many characteristics of cognitive decline might be said to overlap with characteristics ascribed to learning disability. But I don't think this is the place to engage with the complexities of such a debate, and in any case, the realisation that I cared about learning disability pre-dates by many years my partner's parent's diagnosis.

The revelation that I cared about learning disability has its origins in study support work with disabled students that I undertook in the early 2000s at Liverpool Community College (as it was then called). A friend who worked there suggested the job to me as a way of funding my way through a master's degree in popular music. I did not take it because of any conscious predisposition towards caring for learning disability or learning disabled-people. My friend (who, incidentally, has a 30-year-old diagnosis of bipolar disorder – another disability thread) recommended that I apply for the post because they thought I had a suitable disposition. I worked for several years with many disabled students on a variety of vocational courses, though mainly students with labels of specific learning difficulties (SpLD): mostly dyslexia, but also dyscalculia and dyspraxia, as well as other diagnoses which these days fall under the umbrella term of neurodiversity. I qualified as a teacher in post-compulsory education and again as a specialist teacher of students labelled with specific learning difficulties. That led to two jobs that I worked simultaneously: as a dyslexia support tutor and inclusion manager at a Sixth Form College, and as a university lecturer teaching the British Dyslexia Association accredited course I had recently qualified in myself, training other post-compulsory educators in assessment and pedagogies associated with SpLD.

Between 2007 and 2011, I studied for a Doctorate in Education. A large part of my motivation was increasing annoyance and discomfort at the persistent deficit discourse around dyslexia that I encountered everywhere in my professional life: in the way other teachers at the Sixth Form spoke about dyslexia and dyslexic students; in the content and conceptual underpinnings of the British Dyslexia Association course I was delivering; in the abundant psychomedical research literature. There was very little awareness of alternative perspectives to the psychomedical discourse, and I knew nothing of Disability Studies. Nevertheless, I wanted to be an ally to my dyslexic students and to help them change perceptions of dyslexia and dyslexic students within and beyond the College. For my doctoral thesis, we undertook a participatory project centring on their use of social media for literacy and learning. In saying "my thesis", I acknowledge that my studies further bolstered my position of non-disabled privilege and status. However, the aims and outcomes of the project were negotiated with the students. The students were quite overtly political: they wanted to change not just perceptions of dyslexia and dyslexics, but College attitudes and policy towards social media. Importantly, the research was successful in this aim. After we shared our work with the Principal, the College moved from a position of banning social media on its networks to using social media to communicate with students and parents. We cannot claim all the credit for this change, as the College – like many – was already reviewing its position on social media, but we can say that we did help to shift the dial. The students who participated in the research also said it helped change their families' and friends' perspectives on dyslexia. As such, the project realised tangible benefits to the students involved, shifted attitudes and influenced policy and practice (Barden, 2012).

A few months after completing the doctorate in November 2011, I left the Sixth Form and university I was working at for a post at Liverpool Hope University. My work there immersed me in Disability Studies. In 2018, I began researching the history of learning disability. This was again serendipitous, or at least seemed so to me. Prof. David Bolt, Director of the Centre for Culture and Disability Studies (CCDS) at Liverpool Hope, invited me to contribute a chapter to a multi-volume book series on the cultural history of disability he was co-editing with Prof. Robert McRuer (Barden, 2020a). Around the same time, I was awarded a research grant from the British Academy, which stipulated that the project had to use material in the UK Medical Heritage Library. This was an archive of over 66,000 European 19th-century history of medicine texts. I used the funding to initiate a participatory project, with two groups of researchers with learning disabilities – one in Liverpool, one in South Wales – collaboratively analysing, interpreting and creatively responding to the digital archive material. This and similar projects continue. These are the kinds of ways in which I, as a non-disabled Disability Studies scholar, have tried to act as an advocate and ally for disabled people generally and learning-disabled people specifically. Twenty years after my first, serendipitous encounter with learning disability, I recognise my carings both about the concept of learning disability and for people labelled with learning disabilities as a significant part of who I am.

Conclusion

At first glance, it may seem counter-intuitive for a non-disabled academic to claim to write an autocritical history of learning disability. In this chapter, I have tried to justify this claim and thus contextualise the book that follows. I have given a short, reflective, autobiographical account of my relationships with disability generally and learning disability specifically, and made the point that although my set of relationships is unique, at the same time there will be similarities and overlaps with other people's sets of relationships. Same same but different. In giving this account, I have attempted to respond to calls for researchers to state their position relative to their subject matter, whilst noting that these calls come not just from Disability Studies, but are echoed in broader discourses of educational and qualitative research. I have acknowledged that objectifying one's subjectivity in this way is not only a way of bringing some transparency, originality and rigour to the work, but also highlights its ontological and phenomenological dimensions. The ontological dimension is present in my attempt to come to understand the animate, shapeshifting thing we now know as learning disability. The phenomenological dimension is apparent in my consideration of my position in relation to learning disability. That position is not fixed, however. It is a position of being open to learning disability, of being willing to correspond with learning disability, in order to try to come to understand it not just as a concept which applies to some people and not others, but is essential in our understanding of what it means to be human.

Notes

1 Simone Apsis is a prominent UK learning-disabled advocate and campaigner for disabled people's civil and human rights.
2 I recognise the tensions invoked when equating autism with learning disability; this is a topic I return to in more detail later in the chapter, when I discuss my relationships with disability.
3 I looked it up, and there are many delightful collective nouns for penguins including colony, rookery, huddle, tuxedo, raft (if they're swimming) and waddle (if they're . . . waddling).
4 This phrase has often been erroneously attributed to the renowned anthropologist Margaret Mead. Its actual origins are uncertain.

References

Barden, O. (2012) '". . . If We Were Cavemen We'd Be Fine": Facebook as a Catalyst for Critical Literacy Learning by Dyslexic Sixth-Form Students', *Literacy*, 46(3), pp. 123–132. Available at: https://doi.org/10.1111/j.1741-4369.2012.00662.x.

Barden, O. (2020a) 'A Cultural History of Learning Difficulties in the Modern Age', in D.T. Mitchell and S.L. Snyder (eds) *A Cultural History of Disability in the Modern Age*. London: Bloomsbury Publishing, pp. 111–132.

Barden, O. (2020b) 'Demanding Money with Menaces: Fear and Loathing in the Archipelago of Confinement', *Journal of Literary & Cultural Disability Studies*, 14(1), pp. 91–108.

Berger, J. (2014) *The Disarticulate: Language, Disability, and the Narratives of Modernity*. New York: New York University Press.

Bérubé, M. (2016) *The Secret Life of Stories*. New York: New York University Press.

Carlson, L. (2010) *The Faces of Intellectual Disability Philosophical Reflections*. Bloomington, IN: Indiana University Press.

Cook, T. and Inglis, P. (2009) 'Making Our Own Decisions: Researching the Process of "Being Informed" with People with Learning Difficulties', *Research Ethics*, 5(2), pp. 55–64. Available at: https://doi.org/10.1177/174701610900500204.

Duncan, P.M. and Millard, W. (1866) *A Manual for the Classification, Training, and Education of the Feeble-Minded, Imbecile, & Idiotic*. London: Longmans, Green, and Co.

Garland-Thomson, R. (2015) 'Human Biodiversity Conservation: A Consensual Ethical Principle', *The American Journal of Bioethics*, 15(6), pp. 13–15. Available at: https://doi.org/10.1080/15265161.2015.1028663.

Goodey, C.F. (2011) *A History of Intelligence and 'Intellectual Disability': The Shaping of Psychology in Early Modern Europe*. 1st edn. London: Routledge. Available at: https://doi.org/10.4324/9781315564838.

Goodey, C.F. (2016) *Learning Disability and Inclusion Phobia: Past, Present, Future*. 1st edn. London and New York: Taylor and Francis (Routledge Advances in the Medical Humanities). Available at: https://doi.org/10.4324/9780203556658.

Goodley, D. (2014) *Dis/ability Studies: Theorising Disablism and Ableism*. London: Routledge. Available at: https://hope.primo.exlibrisgroup.com/discovery/fulldisplay?docid=cdi_askewsholts_vlebooks_9781134060900&context=PC&vid=44HOP_INST:VU1&lang=en&search_scope=MyInst_and_CI&adaptor=Primo%20Central&tab=Everything&query=any,contains,Goodley,%20D.%20(2014)%20Dis%2Fability%20Studies:%20Theorising%20disablism%20and%20ableism.%20London:%20Routledge.&offset=0 (Accessed: 1 November 2023).

Goodley, D. *et al.* (2021) 'Key Concerns for Critical Disability Studies', *International Journal of Disability and Social Justice*, 1, pp. 27–49. Available at: https://doi.org/10.13169/intljofdissocjus.1.1.0027.

Ingold, T. (2018) *Anthropology and/as Education*. Abingdon, Oxon: Routledge. Available at: https://www.routledge.com/Anthropology-andas-Education/Ingold/p/book/9780415786553 (Accessed: 1 November 2023).

Jarrett, S. and Tilley, E. (2022) 'The History of the History of Learning Disability', *British Journal of Learning Disabilities*, 50(2), pp. 132–142. Available at: https://doi.org/10.1111/bld.12461.

Jaworska, A. (2010) 'Caring and Full Moral Standing Redux', in E.F. Kittay and L. Carlson (eds) *Cognitive Disability and Its Challenge to Moral Philosophy*. Wiley-Blackwell, pp. 369–392.

Linton, S. (1998) 'Disability Studies/Not Disability Studies', *Disability & Society*, 13(4), pp. 525–539. Available at: https://doi.org/10.1080/09687599826588.

Manning, E. (2016) *The Minor Gesture*. Durham, NC: Duke University Press.

McDermott, R., Goldman, S. and Varenne, H. (2006) 'The Cultural Work of Learning Disabilities', *Educational Researcher*, 35(6), pp. 12–17. Available at: https://doi.org/10.3102/0013189X035006012.

McDonagh, P. (2008) *Idiocy: A Cultural History*. 1st edn. Liverpool University Press. Available at: http://www.jstor.org/stable/j.ctt5vjb9k (Accessed: 23 October 2024).

McGilchrist, I. (2012) *The Master and His Emissary: The Divided Brain and the Making of the Western World*. New Haven, CT: Yale University Press.

Oliver, M. (2002) 'Emancipatory Research: A Vehicle for Social Transformation or Policy Development', in *Using Emancipatory Methodologies in Disability Research. 1st Annual Disability Research Seminar*. Great Southern Hotel, Dublin Airport, National Disability Authority & Centre for Disability Studies, University College Dublin. Available at: https://disability-studies.leeds.ac.uk/wp-content/uploads/sites/40/library/Oliver-Mikes-paper.pdf (Accessed: 21 March 2025).

O'Toole, C. (2013) 'Disclosing Our Relationships to Disabilities: An Invitation for Disability Studies Scholars', *Disability Studies Quarterly*, 33(2). Available at: https://doi.org/10.18061/dsq.v33i2.3708.

Packer, M.J. (2017) *The Science of Qualitative Research*. 2nd edn. Cambridge: Cambridge University Press. Available at: https://doi.org/10.1017/9781108264907.

Peim, N. (2018) *Thinking in Educational Research: Applying Philosophy and Theory*. London: Bloomsbury Publishing.

Pring, R. (2000) *Philosophy of Educational Research*. London: Continuum.

Rancière, J. (1991) *The Ignorant Schoolmaster: Five Lessons in Intellectual Emancipation*. Stanford, CA: Stanford University Press.

Russell, B. (1989) *The Problems of Philosophy*. Oxford: Oxford University Press.

Sparrow, R. (2015) 'Imposing Genetic Diversity', *American Journal of Bioethics*, 15(6), pp. 2–10. Available at: https://doi.org/10.1080/15265161.2015.1028658.

Titchkosky, T. (2024) 'Interpretive Methods in Disability Studies: Dyslexia Inflected Inquiry', *Qualitative Inquiry*. Available at: https://doi.org/10.1177/10778004241254394.

Trent, J.W. (1994) *Inventing the Feeble Mind: A History of Mental Retardation in the United States*. Berkeley: University of California Press.

Wolff, J. (2010) 'Cognitive Disability in a Society of Equals', in *Cognitive Disability and Its Challenge to Moral Philosophy*. Chichester: Wiley-Blackwell, pp. 147–159. Available at: https://doi.org/10.1002/9781444322781.ch8.

2 Human *and* Not Fully Human

Introduction

I now begin my examination of what kind of thing learning disability is, and how conceptions of learning disability relate to conceptions of the human, through exploring tensions and contradictions revealed through the binary opposition of human/not fully human. One paradox is that although learning-disabled people are human, they have often been regarded and treated as not fully human. Another is that despite being regarded as not fully human, they have been instrumental in coming to understand what it means to be human. These paradoxes raise questions about the nature of personhood and citizenship, about the nature of learning disability and about the work that conceptions of learning disability do in society.

This book takes a broadly chronological approach to the study of the history of learning disability, beginning in the early 19th century. Of course, people with what we now call learning disabilities did not just spring into being at this point in time. Excellent histories of learning disability stretching back to antiquity have been written (Bolt and McRuer, 2020; Goodey, 2011). Yet this early 19th century starting point is not entirely arbitrary. It is, I think, at this moment that we see learning disability emerge as what the late Canadian philosopher Ian Hacking called an *organising concept* (Hacking, 2004). Organising concepts are those concepts which radically transform our sense of what it means to be a person. They also therefore shape our sense of what is means to not be a person; that is, not fully human. Learning disability emerges as an organising concept through multiple interwoven discourses arising and coming to prominence through the long 19th century, including medicine and psycho-medicine, education, normalcy, institutionalisation, capitalism, colonialism and nationalism. These discourses establish a regime of truth (Simpson, 2018) or metanarrative (Bolt, 2020) of learning disability, which helps to construct norms around intelligence and citizenship, whilst simultaneously cementing learning-disabled peoples'

DOI: 10.4324/9781003411925-2

position as the ultimate outgroup because of their status as not fully human (Goodey, 2016).

The chapter starts with an explanation of organising concepts and their relationship with Michel Foucault's method of historical ontology. It goes on to show how the discursive dehumanisation of people with learning disabilities derives from the philosophy of Humanism. This dehumanisation has a mutually reinforcing relationship with practices of institutionalisation, which rests on the paradoxical human/not fully human divide, exposing the contradictions inherent in the narrative of Christian benevolent humanitarianism that characterised much of the medical and institutional discourse at that time. The paradox and contradictions still haunt popular conceptions of citizenship and personhood to this day.

Learning Disability: An Organising Concept

An *organising concept* is one which radically transforms our sense of what it means to be human. As such, organising concepts also prompt consideration of what it means to be not human, or not fully human. Ian Hacking, who had a particular interest in how phenomena and their associated concepts come in to being, proposed organising concepts in his book *Historical Ontology* (Hacking, 2004). As I noted in the previous chapter, ontology is concerned with the nature of things: what they are like. The method of historical ontology is, then, a way of investigating how things have come into being, and why they are the way they are. In this case, I am concerned with how learning disability has come into being, and what kind of thing it is. So, historical ontology is a useful approach for an attempt to understand what learning disability is; it is a way of co-responding with learning disability as it moves through time.

Hacking's use of the phrase historical ontology acknowledges the origins of the method in the work of Michel Foucault, and in particular *The Archaeology of Knowledge* (Foucault, 1972). Hacking, whilst conceding that the term historical ontology is both somewhat pompous and rather vague – a criticism which has been levelled at much of Foucault's work – nevertheless contends that it represents a useful way of establishing what kinds of things exist, and what makes it possible for them to come into being, by enabling us to illuminate the creation of phenomena and plot their trajectories through interwoven discourses. Foucault's work has frequently been mobilised in Disability Studies, and is particularly germane to the study of learning disability. His considerations of, and investigations into, things like power, authority, surveillance, discipline, punishment, madness, sexuality and transgressive spaces connect with historical and contemporary concerns and themes pertaining to learning disability.

Historical ontology is especially relevant because it pays particular attention to "practices envisaged simultaneously as a technological type of rationality and as strategic games of liberties" (Foucault, 1984: 40), and, as we shall see, notions and rationality and liberty – and strategic denials of liberty – are central to discourses of personhood and learning disability. Historical ontology is also a method used to problematise our relations to things – in our case, learning disability and the human – and to ourselves and other people. In the preceding chapter, I began to problematise my own relationship with disability generally and learning disability specifically; the work of the rest of the book is to continue and expand that self-critique into a broader "historico-critical reflection" (Foucault, 1984) on learning disability and practices associated with it. Historical ontology has political and ethical dimensions in addition to the historical. In using this method, we investigate the historical, or things come about and change through time. This, Foucault called *genealogical*. We examine how *discourses* – which include not just words but actions – make humans, and how humans make themselves. This, Foucault called *archaeological*. In all of this, we remain acutely sensitive to power and resistance, and critique what we are collectively saying, thinking and doing, in order to bring about change. This is the ethical and emancipatory aim of historical ontology (Packer, 2017). I won't continue to use Foucault's terminology, but this combination of genealogical, archaeological and ethical considerations underpins the rest of this book, including the later histories of the present and of the near future (Garland, 2014).[1]

I will use historical ontology to show how the concept of Learning Disability as we now encounter it, in contrast to older conceptualisations, such as the divine or even the unremarkable, was brought into being as a phenomenon, and how it subsequently become an organising concept in Westernised societies: a concept which has radically transformed our sense of what it means to be (or not be) human. Using the method of historical ontology and the tool of the organising concept allows us to go beyond merely asserting that learning disability is socially constructed and instead address the more fundamental question of the kind of thing it is, or at least appears to be. Here I will draw a parallel with Hacking's (2004) exposition of trauma as an organising concept in contemporary culture. Hacking, noting the shift in the meaning of trauma from principally physical – harm done to the body – to the psychic – harm done to the mind – argues that "the story of trauma can be looked at as a sequence of events in the history of psychology and psychiatry. But my concern is the way in which the trauma concept figures in the constitution of selves" (p19). Here trauma is explicitly positioned as an organising concept, since it has moved beyond the realm of psycho-medicine into culture more broadly, influencing how people conceive of themselves and others. Hacking goes on to explicate this history of trauma using the three ontological axes of truth, power and ethics posited by Foucault, showing how the current conception of trauma shapes our everyday lives in, for example, our responses to natural disasters.

We can paraphrase Hacking's argument, substituting the concept *learning disability* for the concept *trauma*. We then need only a few minor alterations to Hacking's prose (substituting educational terms for military ones, for example) to allow learning disability to emerge from Hacking's logic as an organising concept. The first axis is *truth*. Hacking writes about how a certain person might behave in particular ways that appear to signal trauma to us, thanks to the large body of medico-professional knowledge about trauma generated in that field. In other words, there are certain techno-rational truths which dominate our thinking about trauma and our relationships to it. Paraphrasing, we can say that

> there is the person known about, as having a kind of behaviour and sense of self that is produced by learning disability. Today there is a vast body of knowledge in the burgeoning field of learning disability.

The prevalence and influence of these medico-professional, techno-rational truths about learning disability is evident in contemporary scientific, legal and educational discourses which have roots in our starting point, the early 19th century. The second axis to consider is *power*. Here, rather than simply stating the apparently obvious – that people labelled with learning disabilities are subject to power, and largely powerless themselves – Hacking tacitly encourages us to embrace the Foucauldian notions that power is productive rather than merely repressive, and that wherever there is power there is resistance. This generates possibilities: possibilities for self-empowerment and advocacy; for power of victims over abusers; for students to claim reasonable adjustments and other benefits targeted at people labelled with learning disabilities; for justice through the courts and legislature. These are instances of power in relation to institutions and practices. However, in the cultural sphere, the concept of learning disability has immense power that is at work in our lives. This power is evident in moves both to claim learning disability as an identity and to distance oneself from it in defining oneself. The third axis is ethical. At the moral level, Hacking argues, events happening either in the present or in the act of remembering and experienced through trauma exculpate. Trauma is used to explain or excuse an antisocial person, who may also be diagnosed with, for example, post-traumatic stress disorder. In a parallel vein, someone's unusual or undesirable behaviour might be excused or explained away by learning disability. A hundred years ago, such a person might have been labelled with moral imbecility; before that, with foolishness; now with antisocial personality disorder or any of the other myriad diagnoses available in the medical manuals. These moves to exculpate, explain and excuse in effect create new moral beings; people for whom the expectations of what is right differs to what is expected of everybody else. In this way, conceptualisations of learning disability create new moral beings. Learning disability offers not only a new sense of who others are, and why some may be that way, but also produce a new sense of self, of who one is and why one is as one is.

The spectre lurking in our conceptualisations of self, at least in the West, is Humanism. Humanism is a particular way of understanding what human beings ought to be like. The origins of this philosophy stretch back at least to Ancient Greece and began to exert particular influence in European and American philosophy during the 18th-century Enlightenment. Humanism had a profound influence on philosophical, scientific and political thought right through the 19th and 20th centuries, and still does today. In Chapter 5, I will examine an emerging alternative to Humanism known as Posthumanism, and speculate on its significance to learning disability. Before progressing to the present and future, however, I will consider Humanism and how it shaped dehumanising attitudes towards learning disability in the 19th century.

Humanism Dehumanises

Humanism is a way of thinking about what it means to be human. In this school of thought, the human is referenced to a particular, idealised form. This form is epitomised by Leonardo da Vinci's drawing of Vitruvian Man, which he produced around 1490 (Figure 2.1), during the period known as the Renaissance: the rebirth of civilisation after the murky Middle Ages. Whereas previously God had been central to thought, Humanism positioned Man as the measure of all things. The classical ideal of Man is represented in several ways in Vitruvian Man.

Firstly, Man is a man. The ideal human is represented as male, and not female or any gender outside of this binary. Of this we can be fairly certain, given that the nude has male genitalia and a physique that appears stereotypically masculine. This man is tall, slim, muscular and athletic-looking, symmetrical, fair-skinned and so apparently European, with these characteristics serving to communicate a notion of bodily perfection, which brings in train ideas of perfectibility and progress. The notion of Man as the measure of all things is reinforced not only through the idealised proportions of Vitruvian Man's body, but also through the square and circle he is positioned within. His feet rest on, and his fingertips and the crown of his head touch, the lines demarcating these shapes.

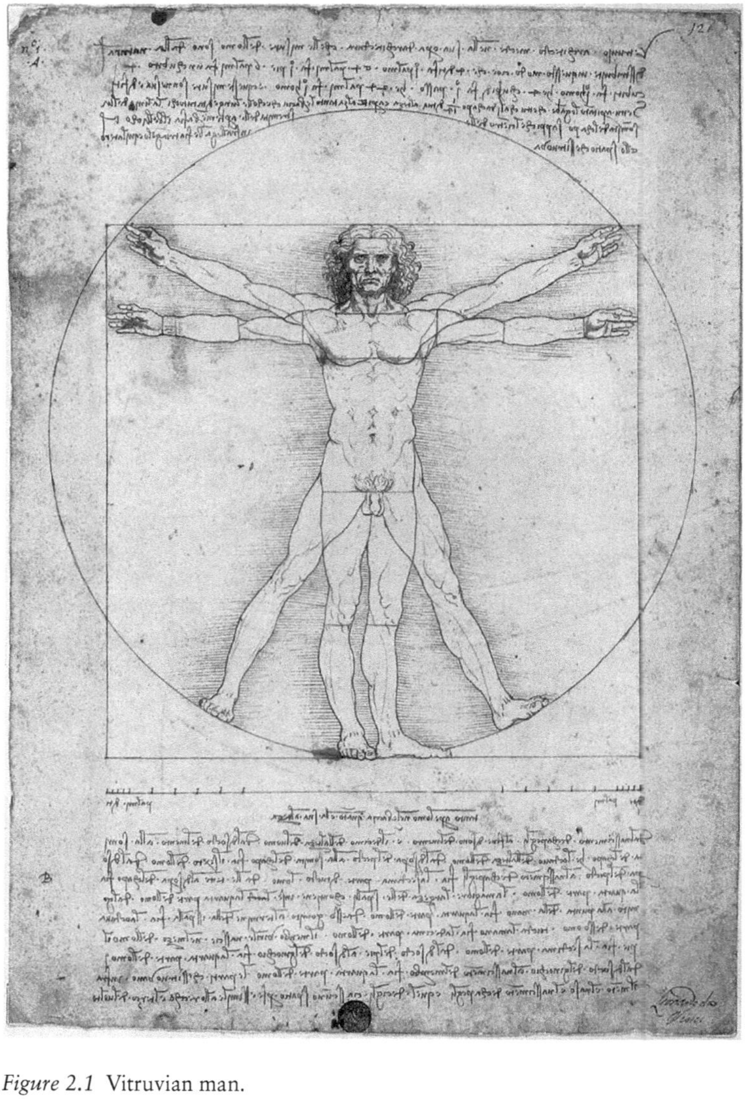

Figure 2.1 Vitruvian man.

The *Vitruvian* in Vitruvian Man's name comes from the Roman architect, engineer and writer Marcus Vitruvius Pollo, and the relationship between the man, the square and the circle can be taken represent his ideas. Vitruvius believed that the proportions of the human body, which he regarded as a microcosm of the universe, should form the basis of all good architecture. This is essentially what the text accompanying the drawing says: it is a detailed translation of Vitruvius' description of the perfectly proportioned human body. The geometric figures of the circle and the square have thus generally been taken to represent either heaven and earth, or divine proportions against which human characteristics and creations ought to be measured (and both are instances of the human replacing God at the centre of thought). However, there is another plausible contemporary reading of these symbols. The square and the circle isolate Vitruvian Man. He stands alone, boxed in. There are no other people in the picture. We can read this as speaking to the Humanist ideal of people being bounded, rational, self-contained, independent, atomistic beings. The idea that people are and should be rational – that is, guided by reason and intellect – capable, responsible, independent and intrinsically moral was and is a central tenant of Humanism, and from it follows our widespread faith in science, reason and capitalism to advance civilisation and solve human problems. For this reason, Vitruvian Man can also be seen to represent a form of intellectual ideal, encapsulated in the Latin phrase *mens sana in corpore sano*: a healthy mind in a healthy body. Roman in origin, this phrase was popularised in the Anglophone world by John Locke's *Some Thoughts Concerning Education*, published in 1693 and a key Enlightenment text.

From this analysis, we can conclude that Vitruvian Man represents not only an ideal, but an inherently ableist ideal of the human. He is an ideal nobody can live up to; no body is as supposedly perfect and symmetrical as his, however much gym bunnies and Instagram influencers might strive for one just like it (Goodley, 2014). We might question the desire for this vision of perfection on grounds other than sheer impossibility. For example, many people would regard the sprinter Usain Bolt as the epitome of athletic perfection. He won eight Olympic gold medals in the 100m and 200m events, was World Champion 11 times in the 100m, 200m and 4×100m relay and set World Records in both the 100m and 200m. His record of 9.58 seconds for the 100m was set in 2009 and still stands. Although he remains a household name because of these achievements, he is not some kind of Jamaican Vitruvian Man. He has scoliosis, which makes his spine curve to the right. So, although he is tall, he is neither straight nor symmetrical. Another effect of scoliosis is that his right leg is half an inch shorter than his left. Conventional scientific wisdom is that a runner's strides should be symmetrical in order to run as quickly and efficiently as possible. However, scientists studying Bolt concluded that his asymmetrical gait enabled him to generate more power, which is the basis of speed, and that "correcting" it to be symmetrical would probably be detrimental (Longman, 2017). We might take this as an example of what Rosemarie Garland-Thomson has dubbed *Disability Gain* (Garland-Thomson, 2013). This concept encourages to appreciate the advantages humans and societies gain from the presence of disability. Few people if any would consider Usain Bolt disabled, yet he probably would not have achieved what he did without his asymmetrical anatomy, and the world would have been deprived a cultural icon.

The notion of a healthy mind in a healthy body might reasonably be interpreted as expressing a desire for a combined physical and an intellectual ideal. It is a normative ideal, dictating how a person should be: fit, capable and smart. As soon as we embrace an ideal like this, we inscribe intelligence (as well as the physical traits) as a cultural value (Goodey, 2011). Intelligence cannot, unlike components of the body, be treated as a physical object for scientific scrutiny: we cannot find it just by looking at the materiality of people's brains. Neither can it be treated as a purely sociological one, even though it becomes a means of establishing status. People don't merely possess intelligence – however it may be defined at any particular moment in time – they strive for more of it, or at least to be perceived as having more of it, because it bestows superior social status. Moreover, intelligence is often quite narrowly defined in terms of capacity for abstract thinking, logical reasoning and speed of thought. The implications of this are perhaps quite obvious. Intelligence – and its perceived lack – becomes fundamental to human relationships and social status and stratification. People deemed unintelligent – because they think too slowly, or are too obviously irrational – are awarded inferior social status. They are seen as less human, or even "less-than-human". In a word, Humanism dehumanises.

In Ancient Greece, the *idiotic* meant the uneducated. Since education was only enjoyed by the privileged few, most people were uneducated. This meant that almost everybody was an idiot, and somewhat like an animal, since they lacked ability to reason. Only over time did the term idiot come to refer, in Europe and America, to a minority of people, and only in the early 19th century did religious causal explanations become fully absorbed into medical ones (Jarrett and Goodey, 2020), as I explore more fully below. I detect here a version of Lennard Davis's argument about broader historical conceptions of disability (Davis, 1995). Up until the Enlightenment, people made a crude distinction between the divine and the grotesque. The divine was the realm of the Gods, and not something ordinary people could attain. Crucially, neither were they expected to. The great mass of humanity – ordinary people – were grotesque and supposed to be that way. There was no shame in it. With the arrival of the Enlightenment came a shift in attitudes. The idea of the normal became conflated with the ideal of the divine, and people were now expected to be as normal – meaning "perfect" – as possible. By the mid-19th century, a certain degree of intelligence was required to qualify as normal and desirable. Yet intelligence was also seen as something people higher up the social hierarchy possessed to a far greater extent than those in lowlier stations. Intelligence is understood as a truly WEIRD phenomenon; it is the property of people coming from Western, Educated, Industrialised, Rich, Democratic countries (Mercier and Sperber, 2018). White, European, male doctors and gentleman scholars represent the intelligent human ideal, and they are the ones with the power and inclination to label and classify others in such a way as to re-inscribe their authority and superiority. It is no coincidence that Vitruvian Man appears just as Christopher Columbus arrives in America. The Humanist ideal helps provide justification not only for the attempted eradication of Native Americans, but also for the horrors of slavery that were to follow. As I will show, fears over "inferior races", whether that inferiority is blamed on skin colour, perceived lack of intellect, or both combined, come to dominant perceptions of learning disability from the mid-19th century onwards. Before that, I will explore a little more deeply conceptualisations of intelligence, and how they have shaped attitudes towards learning disability.

Intelligence, Reason and Reasoning: The Case for Reasoning *with* Learning Disability

The ability to reason is generally regarded as the hallmark of human intelligence; to think logically and in the abstract in order to solve problems is regarded as setting us apart from other animals (Kittay and Carlson, 2010). The conventional view is that reasoning is a solitary activity; something we do in private, inside our own heads, even though in Ancient Greece the argumentative use of reason to convince others was central to understanding both the purpose and quality of reasoning (Mercier and Sperber, 2018). We can align this conventional view of the individual, intelligent reasoner with Vitruvian Man and the Humanist ideal. The conventional view is also, since Darwin, an evolutionary view: that reason must have some biological function which confers an evolutionary advantage, meaning it enhances the chances of reproductive success, otherwise it would have been selected out long ago. Darwin expressed this idea in *The Descent of Man*:

> Of all the faculties of the human mind, it will, I presume, be admitted that *Reason* stands at the summit.
>
> (Darwin, 1871: 46)

It then follows that because intellectual faculties are inherited "they would have been perfected or advanced through natural selection. . . . In the rudest state of society, the individuals who were the most sagacious . . . would rear the greatest number of offspring" (pp 188–189). Such thinking becomes the basis for eugenics, which tries to control who can and who cannot rear children. I will return to the evolutionary view of reason and its implications for learning disability in the next part of this chapter. For the moment, I want to focus on a recent challenge to the individualistic model of intelligence and reason, made by Hugo Mercier and Dan Sperber in *The Enigma of Reason* (Mercier and Sperber, 2018). Their challenge is to do with both the nature and function of reasoning. They take us back to the Socratic view, whilst maintaining an evolutionist standpoint, to argue that reason is interactional, not solitary. Their thesis is that we reason in order to convince others and to evaluate their arguments. The evidence for this position is drawn from a swathe of psychological studies which appear to demonstrate beyond doubt that most people – including even Nobel Prize–winning scientists – appear to be quite poor at solitary logical reasoning, especially of the kind required under experimental conditions. However, as Mercier and Sperber point out, this need not necessarily mean that people are bad at reasoning in real life. There is an echo here of the evidence suggesting that people labelled with learning disabilities – who are likely to have been given their label as a result of performance on standardised psychological tests given under experimental-type conditions – can actually get along perfectly well in many areas of their everyday lives. We will examine the arguments around interactive reasoning in more depth in Chapter 5. For now, the focus remains on critiquing ableist conceptualisations of reasoning.

Contrary to the common-sense picture, much experimental evidence suggests that, far from our beliefs and decisions being based on sound reasons, of which we are cognizant, they are most often intuitive products of our subconscious. We then tend to use reasons to justify or rationalise conclusions we have come to intuitively; we don't usually proceed from a set of reasons to a logical conclusion. Our common-sense view of reason, or rational thought, thus has things the wrong way around. It is on this basis that Mercier and Sperber develop their argument that reasoning is interactional; its function is communicative, in that it enables us to persuade, and we are most persuasive when we use normative justifications and arguments. I would like to make a challenge to Mercier and Sperber's challenge. I am not questioning their claims on the nature and function of reasoning. Rather, I am taking issue with its ableist presumptions. Arguing that reason is a different kind of thing to how we currently understand it, whilst maintaining similar exclusionary criteria to those evident throughout history in relation to learning disability only perpetuates some people's dehumanisation. In our supposedly enlightened and inclusive times, learning disability still appears to be something which disqualifies some people from full personhood. Mercier and Sperber state that "everywhere, people's intuitions about reasons are *anchored in cognitive competencies* that, *too a large extent*, they share as members of the human species" (p143, emphasis added). This can be taken to mean that people deemed "cognitively incompetent" not only lack those competencies, but are not full members of the human species. This position is reflected in the fact that people with learning disabilities continue to be denied many things – marriage, sex and parenthood, to name but a few – because of this perceived lack.

Mercier and Sperber go on to talk about *epistemic vigilance*, by which they mean conscious monitoring of both the source (person) and content (topic) of communications, in order to adjust our level of trust in what we are being told. They make the point (p193):

> An honest communicator may be eager to communicate true and relevant information, but she may not have sufficient authority in the eyes of her interlocutor for him to accept it, in which case they both lose – she in influence, he in the relevant knowledge.

There is a deep irony in them giving this example of a lose-lose situation between one person deemed not to have sufficient authority and another unprepared to re-examine his knowledge and beliefs because of his perception of his interlocutor's inferior status. People with learning disabilities have routinely been silenced and ignored when trying to share their knowledge and lived experience of learning disability, because they are deemed incompetent and untrustworthy and hence having insufficient authority to speak. The irony comes from using this example whilst re-inscribing learning disability – that is, a lack of cognitive competency – as grounds for excluding some people from personhood.

The challenge, then, is to co-respond with learning disability by engaging in dialogue with people with learning disabilities, rather than excluding them from the debate. Responding to this challenge will help address the problem of "people of culture" – to use again Tim Ingold's apt phrase – reasoning *about* learning disability rather than *with* it, and using this reasoning to position learning disability, and learning-disabled people, in very particular ways which fit with their preconceptions and predispositions. People of culture reasoning about, rather than with, learning disability only reinforces subconscious intuitions, which have so far been shaped by hegemonic Humanist ideals. To get a fuller and more accurate and enlightened picture, we need to correspond *with* learning disability and listen to people with learning disabilities. There is an intriguing precedent for this, which returns us to connections between race and learning disability. The abolition of the slave trade in Great Britain was largely the result of two things: abolitionists pointing out in public debates inconsistencies in slavers' justifications for their trade, and the publication of poems and autobiographies written by freed slaves (Mercier and Sperber, 2018). The politicians and the public listened to reason and the voices of the oppressed, and this changed not only minds, but also the law, bringing an official end to a trade that had helped make the country the richest on Earth and could have continued to make it even wealthier.

Another justification for listening to, and reasoning with learning disability is that, as Mercier and Sperber acknowledge, reasoning can lead us to behave immorally, especially if we reason alone or only with like-minded people. Like other aspects of human evolution, reasoning needs not just company but also diversity in order to function well. It is not difficult for a solitary reasoner to come up with reasons that seem to them to justify behaving immorally. We know that one person in four in Britain will avoid conversation with an obviously disabled person, even though one person in five is disabled. Evidence from psychological experiments from as far back as the 1970s shows that non-disabled people will readily produce ad hoc rationalisations for avoiding sitting next to somebody who appears to have a physical impairment, for example (Staniland, 2009; Dixon *et al.*, 2018; Mercier and Sperber, 2018). This might be taken as indicator of how deeply ingrained prejudicial attitudes towards disability are, at least in the kinds of WEIRD places and cultures where such experiments take place. We can trace the origins of such experiments back to the 19th century.

Idiocy and the Human

In the early 19th century, learning disability, in the guise of the idiot, emerges as an object of concerted scientific inquiry and intervention. It appears as an object with the potential to illuminate human nature, to afford non-disabled people opportunities to do what they see as God's work, and – through combining this understanding and these opportunities – contribute to the betterment of society. Despite being regarded as not fully human, idiots are thought to hold the key to scientific understanding of what it means to be human. It is at this moment in history that a network of institutions and professional knowledge, or what Foucault called "a technology of human abnormality" (Foucault, 2003: 61), is established. This network of power and knowledge seeks to control people deemed abnormal not only through physical segregation in specialised locations but also by controlling what is known and said about them. In other words, by controlling the discourse. The network begins to distinguish between the mentally ill, or mad, and the learning-disabled, or idiots, imbeciles and feebleminded. Each "kind" of person, once captured in the spotlight of this surveillance network, is allocated to a particular kind of institution under the control of a particular kind of professional. The physical manifestations of this network have been characterised, after Foucault, as the "archipelago of confinement and control" (Spivakovsky, 2017: 366), scattered as they were across the globe. In the case of idiots, imbeciles and the feebleminded, the islands of this archipelago took a variety of forms, such as special schools, approved schools, hospitals, farm schools, colonies, asylums and reform schools; in the late 1800s, Liverpool even had two reform ships – the Akbar (Protestant) and the Clarence (Catholic) – permanently moored in the docks to house unruly orphans, often prior to transportation (i.e. forced emigration) to North America or Australia. Such islands are established across Europe, the United Kingdom and the United States. This emerging archipelago falls under the control of medical professionals: doctors, psychologists and superintendents, who were invariably men. Up until this point, studies related to idiocy had been case studies of individuals. For example, of feral children like *Juvenis Ovinus Hibernus*, a boy supposedly found living among wild sheep in Ireland, or "Victor", the famous Savage or Wild Boy discovered living in the woods around Aveyron in France. Now, the studies became systematic and connected, and so knowledge of, and responses to, learning disability became coordinated; this is how the power-knowledge network sustains its status.

One particularly influential figure in this network was Edward Seguin (aka Eduoard Séguin). Seguin originally practised at the Salpêtrière and Bicêtre hospitals, as well as privately, in Paris in the earlier part of the 19th century, establishing a favourable reputation on the basis of his publications on methods for "treating" idiots. He emigrated to the United States in 1850 having fallen out with the French authorities. After some initial struggles to reignite his career, he regained his influence in both America and Europe. This was in part due to the translation into English of his treatise *Idiocy and Its Treatment by the Physiological Method* (Seguin, 1866). Seguin's physiological method entailed a progressive curriculum which began by training sensitivity and awareness in the senses, then the intellect, and finally reflection and moral reasoning. His multisensory pedagogy still underpins much inclusive classroom practice today. In developing his method, Seguin was influenced by Jean-Marc Itard, who had himself taught Victor, the Wild Boy of Aveyron. This is where the scientific study of learning disability to better understand human nature comes into play. Unlike his rival physician Philippe Pinel, Itard believed that Victor was not an idiot but simply wild, and therefore represented a kind of Rousseauian *tabula rasa*. Pinel thought Victor simply an idiot and therefore ineducable. Itard tried to educate Victor for a number of years. His frustrations in this endeavour appeared to make him tacitly revise his opinion in the direction of Victor in fact being an idiot (Trent, 1994). However, according to Seguin, Itard's goal in trying to educate Victor was not to benefit Victor; it was to gain a better understanding of human nature:

> [H]is object was not to improve or cure an idiot; it was to solve the metaphysical problem of determining the degree of intelligence and the nature of ideas.
>
> (Seguin, 1866: 27)

As a so-called "true savage", Victor presented as a vehicle who would, in the words of Itard's predecessor Professor Pierre Jospeh Bonaterre,

> furnish to philosophy and natural history important notions on the original constitution of man, and on the development of his primitive faculties; provided that the state of imbecility we have noticed in this child does not offer an obstacle to his instruction.
>
> (Seguin, 1866: 19)

Evident in these statements are beliefs that idiocy offers potential insight into what it means to be human, particularly in relation to nature/nurture debates. There is also foreshadowing of later conceptualisations of idiots, imbeciles and the feebleminded as evolutionary throwbacks. Both these characteristics reflect the contemporary growing interest in anthropology, particularly the type of comparative anthropology that was rapidly becoming the scientific basis for attempting to understanding what it meant to be human, that is, moral and civilised (Gaukroger, 2016). In Bonaterre's remark, there is also optimism that contrary to prevailing medical opinion, people like Victor could be educated. Although we can read this sympathetic, benevolent attitude as the hallmark of the early institutions, the aims of the network were not restricted to charitable education, or education for its' own or the idiots' sake. In *Idiocy and Its Treatment*, for example, Seguin is quite explicit in his belief that professionals like himself are doing divine work in trying to move humanity towards a more perfect society:

> At a given hour, anything wanted by the race makes its appearance simultaneously from so many quarters, that the title of a simple individual to discovery is always contested, and seems clearly to belong to God manifested through man. . . . The origin of the methodical treatment of idiots . . . is one of these necessary events, coming when needed for the co-ordination of progress.
>
> (Seguin, 1866: 9)

Here again is Man as the measure of all things and the associated ideas of perfectibility and progress. This Humanist, anthropological frame of reference was being augmented by emerging evolutionary theory, and here we return to Charles Darwin. Darwin was an extremely influential figure in the history of what we now call learning disability. As we saw earlier in the chapter, he was keen to evoke rational thinking as the pinnacle of human intellectual abilities. Yet he went further than merely advocating for the "most sagacious" people to have the most children, although this is in itself an early argument for what became known as *positive eugenics* (Darwin's cousin, Sir Francis Galton, would not coin the term *eugenics* until in 1883, in his book *Hereditary Genius*).

The picture here is a little complicated by the fact that Darwin married his cousin, Emma Wedgewood, aware that this presented a significant hereditary health risk for any children of theirs. There is evidence to suggest that their tenth and last child, Charles Waring Darwin, was born, in the words of his sister Henrietta, without his "full share of intelligence" (Smith, 1999; Gelb, 2008). Scholars have speculated that this may have been Down's Syndrome, which would have been known at the time as Mongolian idiocy. Darwin's actions here seem to underscore Mercier and Sperber's claim that even very intelligent people often struggle to act rationally. That aside, in order to develop his theory of evolution by natural selection, Darwin relied on dehumanising comparisons between idiots and what he termed the lower animals. In *The Descent of Man*, one of his strategies was to make physical comparisons; because idiots were observed to be fond of climbing furniture and trees, and often ascended stairs on all fours, they were closer to monkeys than people. A second strategy was to make intellectual comparisons, claiming that

> we may trace a perfect gradation from the mind of an utter idiot, lower than that of the lowest animal, to the mind of a Newton.
>
> (Darwin, 1871 quoted in Gelb, 2008: np)

Given that Darwin had studied barnacles and worms, amongst a great many other animals, positioning idiots as the lowest of the low is really quite remarkable, even if he did slightly revise this assessment in the second edition (Gelb, 2008). We should also pause here to note that there were explicitly racial considerations in Darwin's arguments: he hoped that Caucasians would prevail over the savage "negro or Australian" (referring to Aborigines), a sentiment prevalent in anxieties around racial degeneration (McDonagh, 2020). There is a further irony here in that so influential was the pseudoscience of physiognomy that Darwin was almost refused his position on The Beagle because its captain didn't trust the shape of his nose (Gaukroger, 2016). Of course, he did sail and hence develop his theory of evolution by natural selection. Darwin and Galton certainly influenced each other, and we could take their mutually reinforcing positions on learning disability as a prime example of "the dark side of reasoning" (Mercier and Sperber, 2018: 237). Their exchanges helped form a discourse in which, from the early 19th century onwards, professions and institutions of confinement have manipulated perceptions of people with intellectual impairments, and consequently profited as a result of a regime of truth they have helped to construct (Barden, 2020a). Remember that by a *regime of truth*, we mean a powerful set of ideas which define how an object is thought about, or what we might otherwise call a *metanarrative*. Metanarratives are stories about objects which circulate at the cultural level, having been created by those who assume the authority to speak, and which shape our thinking about those objects, whether we are conscious of the metanarrative or not (Bolt, 2020). Under the metanarrative or regime of truth initially constructed by Darwin, Galton and many of their contemporaries, people with intellectual impairments are represented as vulnerable, menacing or risky Others who are not worthy of personhood and thus require control (Barden and Walden, 2021). At the same time, the professions and institutions of confinement assume authority over "the problem" by relocating and segregating stigmatised individuals and assuring the public that "the problem" is under control.

Darwin himself was in favour of asylums, rather than extermination or sterilisation, on the grounds of compassion being one of the finest qualities of a civilised society. This is an example of the kind of benevolent humanitarianism, philanthropy and Christian charity that helped justify the widespread segregation and institutionalisation of idiots, imbeciles and the feebleminded that began in the early 19th century. This move also provides some of those same professionals with captive populations for their own scientific, educational and capitalist endeavours, which were geared either towards enabling people labelled with learning disabilities to approximate norms or towards keeping them segregated from the population considered normal. These processes of measurement, classification and segregation brought into being new kinds of people through taxonomies established about perceived intellectual ability. Here are the origins of ongoing "omnipotent fantasies of medical profession being able to cure and heal everyone" (Kremsner *et al.*, 2021: 36) However, the method of historical ontology permits us to see the emergence of learning disability as an organising concept and a cause for existential concern not simply as the result of the writings of a small but influential number of "great men" like Seguin, Darwin and Galton but as a product of a discursive field comprising medicine, education, social Darwinism and social work, scientism in a context of continuing urbanisation and population growth, expansionism, capitalism, colonialism, nationalism and, as a forerunner of today's neoliberalism, a metanarrative of individualised, meritocratic success (Barden, 2020b).

Conclusion

In this chapter, I have introduced the method of historical ontology and the tool of the organising concept to show how learning disability emerges as a specific concern in the mid-19th century. Its emergence is founded on a particular philosophy of what it means to be human, called Humanism, which exerts a strong normative influence on considerations of what a person should be like and be able to do. One important effect of Humanism is to dehumanise those people who, on grounds of race, ascribed lack of intelligence, or both, do not meet the Humanist ideal. This dehumanisation is produced through discourse and serves to perpetuate and reinforce the outgroup status of dehumanised groups, justifying prejudice, stigma and coercive control, often through segregation and institutionalisation and sometimes through other means, including sterilisation and extermination. What can we learn from learning disability in all this? For one thing, learning disability provides an example not just of how concepts and associated attitudes are socially, culturally and historically constructed, but of how we can come to know both the processes by which they are constructed, and the character of those constructions. In this case, learning disability appears first as an object of curiosity, then of scientific inquiry, and then pity and charity. As we shall see in the next chapter, within a few decades, it mutates in an object of existential terror.

Learning disability also helps demarcate the limits of and paradoxes our thinking about intelligence and personhood. On the one hand, the Humanist notion of intelligence marks those with intellectual impairments as an outgroup, and culture and discourse work hard to maintain this status. Yet paradoxically, this outgroup appears to hold the key to understanding what it means to be human. On the other hand, as Darwin's case shows, people can and do love the very people the dominant discourse – a discourse we may ourselves have helped to build – tells us we should reject, ostracise and eliminate. We care about them. Darwin wrote beautifully and tenderly about his intellectually impaired namesake son, Charles Waring, even when his own theory would have denounced him as nothing more than an evolutionary throwback. What we might learn from this is that our conception of the human should not be bound to a notion of intelligence, at least not of the kind measured by psychologists' tests. Perhaps a capacity to care for and about others should be given more weight than notions of intelligence in our considerations of what it means to be human.

Note

1 These may seem like oxymorons, but in Foucault's conceptualisation a "history of the present" means using historical ontology to re-evaluate contemporary phenomena.

References

Barden, O. (2020a) 'A Cultural History of Learning Difficulties in the Modern Age', in D.T. Mitchell and S.L. Snyder (eds) *A Cultural History of Disability in the Modern Age*. London: Bloomsbury Publishing, pp. 111–132.

Barden, O. (2020b) 'Demanding Money with Menaces: Fear and Loathing in the Archipelago of Confinement', *Journal of Literary & Cultural Disability Studies*, 14(1), pp. 91–108.

Barden, O. and Walden, S.J. (2021) 'The Metanarrative of Learning Disability', in D. Bolt (ed) *Metanarratives of Disability: Culture, Assumed Authority, and the Normative Social Order*. Abingdon, Oxon: Routledge, pp. 77–93.

Bolt, D. (2020) 'The Metanarrative of Disability: Social Encounters, Cultural Representation and Critical Avoidance', in N. Watson and S. Vehmas (eds) *Routledge Handbook of Disability Studies*. 2nd edn. Abingdon, Oxon: Routledge.

Bolt, D. and McRuer, R. (eds) (2020) *A Cultural History of Disability*. London and New York: Bloomsbury Publishing (Cultural History). Available at: https://www.bloomsbury.com/uk/cultural-history-of-disability-9781350029538/ (Accessed: 2 November 2023).

Darwin, C. (1871) *The Descent of Man*. Princeton, NJ: Princeton University Press.

Davis, L.J. (1995) *Enforcing Normalcy: Disability, Deafness and the Body*. New York: Verso.

Dixon, S., Smith, C. and Touchet, A. (2018) *The Disability Perception Gap*. Scope. Available at: https://www.scope.org.uk/campaigns/disability-perception-gap (Accessed: 18 October 2024).

Foucault, M. (1972) *The Archaeology of Knowledge*. London: Tavistock Publications.

Foucault, M. (1984) 'What Is Enlightenment?', in P. Rabinow (ed) *The Foucault Reader*. Pantheon Books, pp. 32–50. Available at: https://foucault.info/documents/foucault.whatIsEnlightenment.en/.

Foucault, M. (2003) *Abnormal: Lectures at the College de France*. New York: Picador.

Garland, D. (2014) 'What Is a "History of the Present"? On Foucault's Genealogies and Their Critical Preconditions', *Punishment & Society*, 16(4), pp. 365–384. Available at: https://doi.org/10.1177/1462474514541711.

Garland-Thomson, R. (2013) 'Disability Gain', in *Avoidance and the Academy International Conference on Disability, Culture, and Education*. Liverpool: Centre for Culture and Disability Studies, Liverpool Hope University.

Gaukroger, S. (2016) *The Natural and the Human: Science and the Shaping of Modernity, 1739–1841*. Oxford: Oxford University Press. Available at: https://elib.tcd.ie/login?url=https://search.ebscohost.com/login.aspx?direct=true&db=nlebk&AN=1107416.

Gelb, S.A. (2008) 'Darwin's Use of Intellectual Disability in the Descent of Man', *Disability Studies Quarterly*, 28(2). Available at: https://doi.org/10.18061/dsq.v28i2.96.

Goodey, C.F. (2011) *A History of Intelligence and 'Intellectual Disability': The Shaping of Psychology in Early Modern Europe*. 1st edn. London: Routledge. Available at: https://doi.org/10.4324/9781315564838.

Goodey, C.F. (2016) *Learning Disability and Inclusion Phobia: Past, Present, Future*. 1st edn. London and New York: Taylor and Francis (Routledge Advances in the Medical Humanities). Available at: https://doi.org/10.4324/9780203556658.

Goodley, D. (2014) *Dis/ability Studies: Theorising Disablism and Ableism*. London: Routledge. Available at: https://hope.primo.exlibrisgroup.com/discovery/fulldisplay?docid=cdi_askewsholts_vlebooks_9781134060900&context=PC&vid=44HOP_INST:VU1&lang=en&search_scope=MyInst_and_CI&adaptor=Primo%20Central&tab=Everything&query=any,contains,Goodley,%20D.%20(2014)%20Dis%2Fability%20

Studies:%20Theorising%20disablism%20and%20ableism.%20London:%20Routledge.&offset=0 (Accessed: 1 November 2023).

Hacking, I. (2004) *Historical Ontology*. Cambridge, MA: Harvard University Press.

Jarrett, S. and Goodey, C.F. (2020) 'Learning Difficulties: Intellectual Disability in the Long Eighteenth Century', in D.C. Gabbard and S.B. Mintz (eds) *A Cultural History of Disability in the Long Eighteenth Century*. London: Bloomsbury Publishing, pp. 121–137.

Kittay, E.F. and Carlson, L. (2010) *Cognitive Disability and Its Challenge to Moral Philosophy*. Chichester: Wiley-Blackwell.

Kremsner, G., Koenig, O. and Buchner, T. (2021) 'Tracing the Historical and Ideological Roots of Services for People with Intellectual Disabilities in Austria', in *Intellectual Disability in the Twentieth Century: Transnational Perspectives on People, Policy and Practice*. Bristol: Policy Press, pp. 35–49.

Longman, J. (2017) 'Something Strange in Usain Bolt's Stride', *The New York Times*, 20 July. Available at: https://www.nytimes.com/2017/07/20/sports/olympics/usain-bolt-stride-speed.html (Accessed: 7 December 2023).

McDonagh, P. (2020) 'Learning Difficulties: The Transformation of "Idiocy" in the Nineteenth Century', in J.L. Huff and M. Stoddard Holmes (eds) *A Cultural History of Disability in the Long Nineteenth Century*. London: Bloomsbury Publishing, pp. 129–147.

Mercier, H. and Sperber, D. (2018) *The Enigma of Reason: A New Theory of Human Understanding*. Great Britain: Penguin Books.

Seguin, E. (1866) *Idiocy: And Its Treatment by the Physiological Method*. New York: William Wood & Co.

Simpson, M.K. (2018) *Modernity and the Appearance of Idiocy: Intellectual Disability as a Regime of Truth*. New York and Lampeter: Edwin Mellen Press.

Smith, D.J. (1999) 'Darwin's Last Child: Mental Retardation and the Need for a Romantic Science', *Mental Retardation*, 37(6), pp. 504–506. Available at: https://doi.org/10.1352/0047-6765(1999)037<0504:DLCMRA>2.0.CO;2.

Spivakovsky, C. (2017) 'Governing Freedom Through Risk: Locating the Group Home in the Archipelago of Confinement and Control', *Punishment & Society*, 19(3), pp. 366–383. Available at: https://doi.org/10.1177/1462474517703968.

Staniland, L. (2009) *Public Perceptions of Disabled People: Evidence from the British Social Attitudes Survey 2009*. London: HM Government Office for Disability Issues. Available at: https://assets.publishing.service.gov.uk/media/5a7ed23be5274a2e87db21ea/ppdp.pdf (Accessed: 18 October 2024).

Trent, J.W. (1994) *Inventing the Feeble Mind: A History of Mental Retardation in the United States*. Berkeley: University of California Press.

3 Vulnerable *and* Menacing

Introduction

This chapter moves from the mid-19th century to the early 20th century. It charts the shift in perceptions of people with learning disabilities from being perceived as excessively vulnerable, and therefore requiring care and protection, to being considered menaces requiring permanent segregation and even elimination. This shift is one example of how the "thing" now known as learning disability has changed its meaning as it moves through time, and of how such changes in meaning reflect conceptions of what it means to be human. From the mid-19th century onwards, professions and institutions of confinement simultaneously stoked and assuaged emotions towards people marked with intellectual or cognitive impairments. In doing so, they cemented their subjects' status as the ultimate outgroup, imprisoning them in a regime of truth constructed from interlocking medical, psychological, pedagogical, moral, religious, humanitarian and political discourses relating to the normative functioning of minds, bodies and development (Carlson, 2010; Simpson, 2018). Whether people with learning disabilities are discursively positioned as vulnerable or menacing, the newly established professions and institutions of confinement assume authority and maintain control over "the problem" by relocating and segregating stigmatised individuals and assuring the public that "the problem" is under control. Meanwhile, processes of measurement and classification bring into being new kinds of people through taxonomies based upon perceived intellectual ability. In this way, "normalization becomes one of the great instruments of power at the end of the classical age" (Foucault quoted in Ball, 2012: 54). We see here the origins of current "concerted activities of millions of people engaging in a surveillance system consisting of professionals – doctors, psychologists, lawyers, educators – and parents" (McDermott *et al.*, 2006: 213) which operate in relation to learning disability. To illustrate this shift from vulnerable to menacing, the chapter initially examines the changes in definitions and diagnoses associated

DOI: 10.4324/9781003411925-3

with learning disability, before exploring the invention of the moron by Henry H. Goddard. Goddard was a prominent American psychologist in the early 20th century, who gained considerable fame as the author of the 1912 *Kallikak Family* study. Goddard's work provides an excellent example of both the myth of the disinterested scientist and the way conceptualisations of learning disability reflect and refract contemporary conceptualisations of the human.

From Vulnerable to Menacing

The early institutions presented themselves as caring for the vulnerable, just as today people with learning disabilities are often described as being at greater risk of exploitation or maltreatment than other people. In the Introduction to *Idiocy and Its Treatment,* Edouard Seguin relays a speech given by one Rev. Samuel J. May at the ceremonial laying of the cornerstone of the first, privately funded, school built for idiots in the United States, at Syracuse in the state of New York. May has hitherto worried over "how the Good God, the Heavenly Father, could permit his children of the earth to be so tempted, tried and afflicted as they were" and over "idiocy so appalling in its appearance, so hopeless in its nature" (quoted in Seguin, 1866: 10–11). At the same ceremony, the prominent social reformer Samuel Gridley Howe, who helped set up the Massachusetts School for Idiot and Feeble-Minded Youth, the first such state-funded institution in America, declared idiots to be "a class far, far more deplorably afflicted" (Seguin, 1866: 12) than deaf mutes, blind people and the insane. The idea that people with intellectual disabilities needed protecting, whether from their own temptations, their afflictions or exploitation by others, was also present in definitions of idiocy. Seguin's own definition included the assertion that

> the idiot moves, feels, understands, wills, but imperfectly; does nothing, thinks of nothing, cares for nothing (extreme cases), he is a minor legally irresponsible; isolated, without associations; a soul shut up in imperfect organs, an innocent.
>
> (Seguin, 1866: 39)

The first clause denotes the idiot as incomplete and so imperfect. The second clause reflects the perception of the idiot as a tabula rasa; an empty slate, lacking the volition to learn or even to act. The later clauses liken the idiot to a child: a minor, an innocent. All this paints a picture of vulnerability. Against a backdrop of philanthropy and Christian benevolent humanitarianism, the nodes of the archipelago of control are thus figured as places which exist to protect the excessively vulnerable. Over in the UK, Dr Telford Telford-Smith and Dr William Henry Coupland, both considered experts at the time, were involved in setting up a charity to support the newly established Edinburgh Home and School for Invalid and Imbecile Children. In 1856, they co-authored a promotional pamphlet which proclaimed:

> Never has an infant charity made such progress in such a short period. Never has a board of similar character taken up such serious responsibilities; and never, perhaps, has any one been so sustained by public sympathy. . . . The benefit has already extended beyond the sphere of our exertions. The tone of public feeling in relation to the poor idiot has been raised. He can never again be the forlorn abandoned, scorned, imprisoned creature he once was.
>
> (Telford-Smith and Coupland, 1856: 9)

They present the work of the institution as a *serious responsibility* arising from *public sympathy* for the *poor idiot.* The poor idiot is *forlorn, abandoned* and *scorned*, which is to say vulnerable to neglect and abuse. The claim to be freeing the poor idiot from imprisonment is a curious one, given that the Edinburgh institution and others like it were expressly designed to segregate their target populations. Perhaps the statement reflects the initial intention for inmates to only spend short stays in such places before taking their place in the outside world, having been educated or trained in a vocation. Perhaps it reflects a sentiment that idiots and imbeciles were more likely to be convicted of a crime and hence sent to prison, a fate from which the institution would save them. Or perhaps it reflects a metaphorical imprisonment; previously forlorn and abandoned, the poor idiot was no longer inescapably trapped in pitiful circumstances. Although we cannot be sure of the intended meaning here, what is clear is that the passage invokes paints a picture of vulnerability, from which idiots are being rescued. This apparent rehabilitation of the idiot itself represents a shift in attitudes. Etymologically, *idiot* derives from the Ancient Greek *idios*, meaning "one's own", and which referred to someone deemed self-centred unable to reason or self-regulate, and therefore ineducable and contributing nothing to the common good. Although idiots might have been tolerated in the preceding centuries (Jarrett, 2020), these strategic moves to rehabilitate and socialise them, by creating productive members of society – within a Humanist frame of perfectibility – appear to be a new development.

These charitable ideals did not last long, however. Governments and institutions soon sought to confine and control the lives of people labelled with what we now call learning disabilities. Rather than protecting the vulnerable from society, institutions instead came to protect society from its undesirables. The interests of medical and educational professionals, seeking to define and protect their territory, and ensure careers and income, synergised with the interests of capitalist governments newly concerned with productivity, efficiency, Imperialism and racial hygiene. This shift largely removed the goal of creating productive members of society from the "feebleminded" classes, replacing it with one of containment which is still in place today. Colonies, farm schools, asylums and the like sought to become self-sufficient and self-contained: not only through growing and making their own food, clothes and so on, but also by training the "higher grade" inmates to care for their "lower grade" peers. This isolation served governments preoccupied with Imperialist agendas and maximising productivity and wealth by keeping undesirables away from the rest of the population and – through strict surveillance, gender segregation and, sometimes, sterilisation – unable to have children, and thereby helping, it was thought, to maximise the health, fitness and productivity of the nation. This shift in attitude and purpose is evident in, for example, the records of the Royal Albert Asylum for Idiots and Imbeciles of the Seven Northern Counties, held in the Lancashire County Archives. This large asylum existed near Lancaster in England. The first 50 patients were admitted in December 1870. They were children aged 5–16. The normal maximum length of stay was seven years. In 1909, out of a total of 662 patients, 563 (85%) were aged under 15. By 1948, when the Royal Albert was incorporated as a hospital into the newly formed National Health Service, there were 886 patients, of whom only 107 (12%) were aged under 15. The original ratio of children to adults had become inverted. The purpose of the Royal Albert had changed from educating children to warehousing adults deemed incapable of living in the community (Alston, 1992).

Meanwhile, technologies of learning – literacy, writing, grading and examination – were being developed as forms of accountancy, discipline and differentiation, means of both measuring and recording learners and distributing them into specialist locations with a "grammocentric world" (Ball, 2012: 47). Tom Campbell describes the ways in which such technologies enabled governments towards the end of the 19th century to see inside their citizens' heads, to know what each individual knew and did not know, could do and could not do, as never before, and thus intervene to control their populations by emplacing individuals according to their academic performance (Campbell, 2013). Such educational surveillance technologies lay the foundations not only for stigmatisation, regulation and government of the self, but also for the eugenics movement and its ultimate appalling expression in the genocidal Nazi Aktion T4 programme (Snyder and Mitchell, 2006).

As nodes of this network, agents of this discursive regime, the new institutions and professions of rehabilitation (Stiker, 1999) made "mental deficiency" or "feeblemindedness" more visible and helped turn it into a national concern. There was a concomitant shift from a pathetic to a more menacing image of learning disabilities, aided and abetted by isolationist practices (which helped to foster a sense of Otherness), the eugenicist move towards confirming intelligence as hereditary, desirable and manipulable, and the medical professions constituting themselves as experts on the problem of mental deficiency, writing and discussing articles and books in which feeblemindedness was likened to an organic disease (Digby, 1996). As such, the rise of Georgian and Victorian institutions, and of segregated education systems, was driven more by the desire to safeguard the interests of society than to care for or educate the people within them. This desire, evident in the popularity of the eugenics movement generally, and specifically in the invention of the moron discussed in the final section of this chapter, can still be discerned within the archipelago of control today.

The shift in attitudes can also be traced through the evolving definitions of learning disability. In 1866, Seguin had defined idiocy in terms of innocence. In 1908, the British Royal Commission on the Care and Control of the Feeble-Minded adopted the following definitions of classes of mental defect:

> "Idiots" i.e. persons so deeply defective in mind from birth or from an early age, that they are unable to guard themself against common physical dangers, such as, in the case of young children, would prevent their parents from leaving them alone.
>
> "Imbeciles" i.e. persons who are capable of guarding themselves against common physical dangers, but who are incapable of earning their own living by reason of mental defect existing from birth or from an early age.
>
> "Feeble-minded" i.e. persons who may be capable of earning a living under favourable circumstances, but are incapable, from mental defect existing from birth or from an early age, (a) of competing on equal terms with their normal fellows; or (b) of managing themselves and their affairs with ordinary prudence.
>
> "Moral imbeciles" i.e. persons who from an early age display some mental defect coupled with strong vicious or criminal propensities on which punishment has little or no deterrent effect.
>
> Royal Commission on the Care and Control of the Feeble-Minded (1908: 108)

The first three classifications are given in terms of "risk" of harm to the person, echoing Seguin. However, appended to these was the new class of the moral imbecile. This fourth classification reflects the invigorated moral connotations of perceived mental deficiency through emphasising the imperative to protect society from crime and degeneracy rather than, as with the preceding three, conceits of protecting people portrayed as vulnerable. The invention of this new category of person is something we shall return to in more detail in the final section of this chapter.

Before that, two examples might serve to illustrate the ways in which, over the course of just a few decades, the discourse of vulnerability and care was replaced by one of menace and control.

James B.B. and Nellie F. in the Royal Albert Asylum near Lancaster, England

In 1864, James Brunton, a Quaker businessman, offered Dr Edward Dennis de Vitre, visiting physician at the Lancashire County Lunatic Asylum, £2000[1] to establish in Lancashire an asylum for idiots and imbeciles (Alston, 1992). De Vitre formed a Committee who immediately set about fundraising for the Royal Albert Asylum for Idiots and Imbeciles of the Seven Northern Counties. They were extremely successful. Queen Victoria granted patronage and donated 100 guineas, the equivalent of £6,600 in today's money. Seguin himself visited in 1873. Its Medical Superintendents included the notable figures of George Edward Shuttleworth and the aforementioned W.H. Coupland. Religious, psycho-medical and educational discourses combined to present a narrative of benevolence, acceptance and the potential for "improvement", with an initial emphasis on education. In line with Seguin's physiological method, there was "scholastic" classroom education involving singing and exercises; tuition in literacy, numeracy and drawing; and gender-specific training in trades such as shoemaking, tailoring, joinery, laundry, farming and needlework. There was also physical training under the instruction of a Gymnastic Master. Although philanthropy from the rich was significant source of funding, much of the money came from subscriptions and donations from ordinary people, generated through concerted appeals to the public's sentiments of sympathy, pity and charity. All told, in the 41 years to 1906 (the tenure of the Royal Albert's first Secretary), £468,000 was donated to the institution, equivalent to £37–40 million today. Paternalistic Christian philanthropy and benevolent humanitarianism, epitomised in verses included in the early reports of the Royal Albert's annual meetings, were the guiding philosophies:

> *God help the Imbecile! More dark their lot*
> *Than dumb, or deaf, the cripple, or the blind;*
> *The closed soul vision theirs; the blighted mind;*
> *Babes though full grown; the page of life a blot*
>
> *Yet say, shall their affliction be abhorred?*
> *Their need o'er looked? Shall charity pass by?*
> *Leave them to perish with averted eye?*
> *Forbid the love that burns to save her Lord!*
>
> (Alston, 1992: 2)

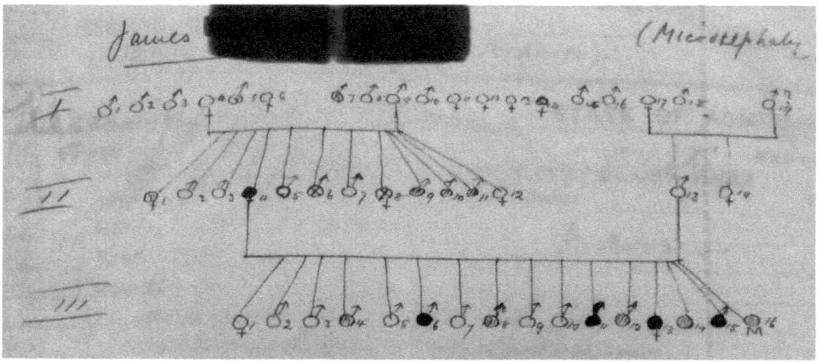

Figure 3.1 Hand-drawn family tree of James B.B. in the Royal Albert admissions book.

Echoing *The Descent of Man*, Sanguin and Howe, the verses clearly locate imbeciles at the bottom of the hierarchy of disability: imbeciles' lives are little more than mistakes – blots – and they themselves little more than children – *babes though full grown* – who nevertheless are not to be abhorred or overlooked by Christian love. The patient records of the Royal Albert, however, held at the Lancashire County Archive, provide a different perspective on the philosophy and work of the institution. The "case books" are huge leather-bound tomes which contain admissions information, diagnoses and detailed patient histories. Many begin with intricate, hand-drawn genealogies with codes and notes on family members' undesirable characteristics. Figure 3.1 shows a photograph of the family tree of James B.B., who was admitted with a diagnosis of microcephalic idiocy. This means idiocy caused by having an exceptionally small head. The different shadings in the circles represent particular points of interest to the tree's creator, probably Coupland. For example, the solid black circles in the second and third rows signify "mental deficiency", whilst the crosses in numbers six and eight in the second row signify insanity and suicide.

Many of the entries also have portrait photographs, itself remarkable given that photography was a such a new technology at the time. It is easy to speculate that these portraits served more than a mere documentary or decorative function, and would have been appropriated for physiognomological analysis. As we progress through the case books to the early 20th century, we begin to find the results of Binet–Simon intelligence tests included as well, along with the resulting diagnoses. The diagnoses would have determined the ward, education and work the patients would be allocated to. Figure 3.2 shows a photograph of the admissions data for patient Nellie F. Dated 20 June 1910, it starts with a History, which records that mental deficiency was first observed

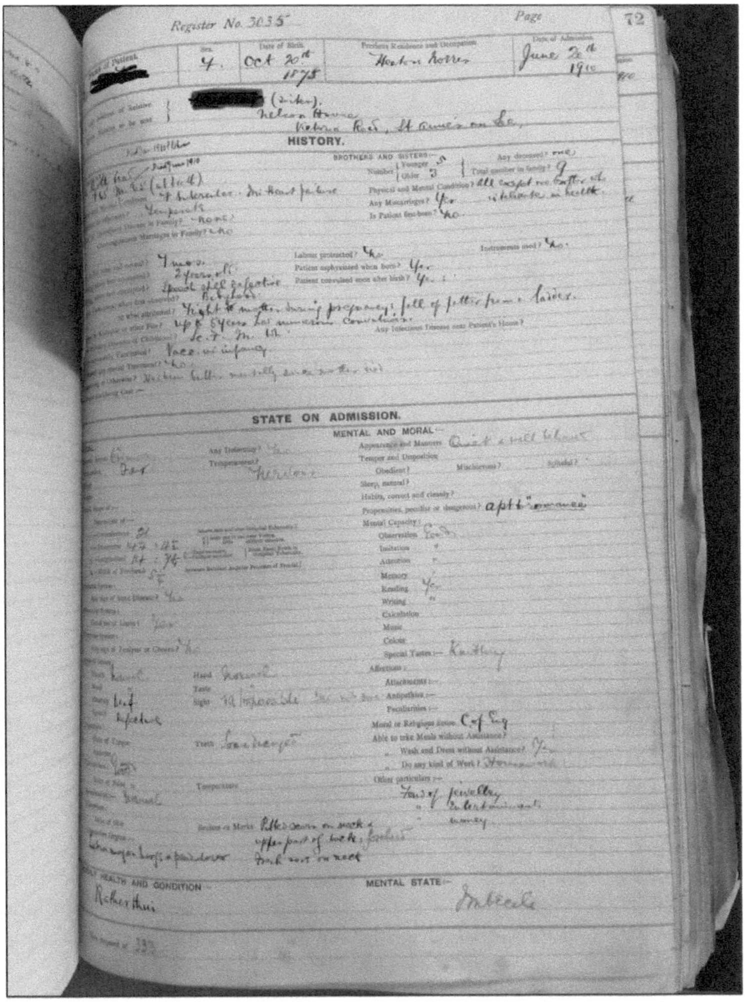
Register No. 3035

Page 72

Sex. F. Date of Birth Oct 20th 1875

Date of Admission June 2nd 1910

[redacted] (sister).

HISTORY.

BROTHERS AND SISTERS

STATE ON ADMISSION.

MENTAL AND MORAL

HEALTH AND CONDITION

MENTAL STATE

Figure 3.2 The Royal Albert admission record for Nellie F., redacted to conceal her full name.

in babyhood, and was attributed to a "fright to mother during pregnancy" and the "fall of father from a ladder". It goes on to record Nellie's State on Admission. This is divided into *Physical* and *Mental & Moral*. Physical includes cranial measurements as well as observations regarding physical health and sensory acuity, as well as temperament. For example, under *Physical*, Nellie is described as nervous, with normal touch and smell but defective speech, and deaf.[2] Under *Mental & Moral*, there are assessments of things like *Appearance and Manners* – Nellie is characterised as "Quiet and well behaved" – and various measures of mental capacity, such as skills in observation, imitation, reading and writing. Some parts of the description read somewhat strangely to modern eyes, with a mixture of the intimate and coy; for example, Nellie is recorded under *Propensities, peculiar or dangerous* as "*Apt to Romance*" and then the size and shape of her genitals is recorded, meaning an intimate physical investigation must have been performed: "Labia majora large and pendulous". The left-hand pages of the ledgers are used for detailed case notes; for most, these are updated only annually, but occasionally there is more consistently detailed reporting, as with Nellie, whose record extends over several pages of the ledger. She died in the Royal Albert on 30 December 1943, having spent over 33 years inside. Nellie thus provides an excellent example of the shift away from short, educative stays in institutions to long-term warehousing.

Antonia Grandoni in Milan, Italy

Antonia Grandoni features prominently as a case history in Dr William W. Ireland's book *On Idiocy and Imbecility* (Ireland, 1877). Dr Ireland was a prominent figure in the study and training of people called mental defectives at that time. Wellcome Collection in London holds a copy of Seguin's *Idiocy and Its Treatment* which has both Ireland's and W.H. Coupland's names handwritten in the flyleaves, indicating that they both owned it at some point and perhaps even swapped it between them. This is further evidence of the professional power-knowledge regime discussed in Chapter 2 and earlier in this chapter. At the time of the publication of Antonia's story, Ireland was Medical Superintendent of the Scottish National Institution for the Education of Imbecile Children at Larbert, Stirlingshire, Scotland. This was one of the first institutions in Scotland to "care" for children labelled with what we now call learning disabilities. As its name suggests, it took children from across the country.

To construct his case study of Antonia Grandoni, Ireland combined a translation of the accounts of one Professor Cardoni, who seems to have taken an interest in Antonia while she was alive, with the post-mortem report of five Italian doctors, and his own observations and interpretations. Ireland devotes 13 pages to Antonia, and this length is perhaps significant in itself – Ireland's account is actually shorter than the Italian doctors', which he says ran to 20 pages. Antonia was clearly of considerable interest to the profession. Her case is partly biographical, giving some details about her life both before and during her life in an unnamed hospital in Milan. There are also two pencil portraits of Antonia, one in profile and the other in three-quarter profile (Figure 3.3).

Figure 3.3 Portrait of Antonia Grandoni.

There are tables containing many measurements, mainly of the size of her face, head and brain, but also including her height and weight. Antonia was one of several children, with her siblings apparently being "quite healthy in every respect". It was noted early in her life that she was small, and with a particularly small head. As she grew older, she "took to wandering about" and evidently this became a concern, especially because she was "fond of learning amorous poetry, and showed erotic tendencies". Owing to these concerns, "At last she was removed to the hospital". It is not said when this happens, but we are told that she has regular periods, which indicates at least adolescence. We also know that she died of blood poisoning in the hospital in 1872, aged 41. This suggests that, like Nellie, she may have been an inmate for a long time. The reason given for Antonia's institutionalisation is a diagnosis of microcephalic idiocy, the same diagnosis given to James B.B. in the Royal Albert. This form of idiocy is attributed to the individual having an exceptionally small head, hence a small brain, and thus reduced intelligence. This explains the tables of measurements, and also the portraits, where Antonia is shown with a shaved head. This may have been routine practice to deter lice and promote hygiene – we can only speculate – but it also emphasises Antonia's physiology and physiognomy. She is wearing a black and white striped jersey, of the kind we might associate with a prison uniform. When researchers with learning disabilities have co-analysed these portraits and the rest of Antonia's story, they have been quick to point out how dehumanising the portrayals are objecting vociferously to the ways the medical men have treated her much like a laboratory rat: as an object to study for their own selfish interests and to advance their careers, rather than as a person in her own right (Barden *et al.*, 2022).

There are some striking similarities in Nellie and Antonia's cases. Both appear to have spent a number of decades in their respective institutions. Neither appears to have benefitted from an education: although being many pages long, Nellie's case only reports on things like her physical health, moods and behaviours, whilst with Antonia, "every attempt to instruct her was without success" (Ireland, 1877: 107). There is also in both cases a very evident concern with sexuality, despite Nellie being of *nervous disposition* and Antonia being *quiet and obedient*. Nellie is *Apt to Romance*, a propensity which qualifies as peculiar and/or dangerous. Antonia is reported as having regular periods and being *fond of learning amorous poetry and showed erotic tendencies . . . fond of attracting the attention of the opposite sex*. Ireland goes on to claim that he would have been able to repress Antonia's erotic tendencies. This belies concerns with reproduction by undesirables and the potential degeneration of the human race. These eugenic concerns had been amplified by Charles Darwin's theory of evolution. Microcephaly was of particular interest to Darwin: he believed that microcephalic idiots represented a reversion to an ancestral form of the human we had now largely evolved beyond. As such these idiots could not be considered fully human; they were merely a missing link between ancient primates and modern Man (Smith, 1999; Gelb, 2008). This helps to explain the anxiety over Antonia's periods, erotic tendencies and fondness of company, amorous poetry, music and dancing. Owing to these anxieties, great pains were taken by the authorities to prevent Antonia, Nellie and a great many people like them from having sex and children, most often through institutionalisation. Sometimes, however, the threat to the State and indeed the human race was deemed so great that even more drastic measures were called for, including systematic extermination (McDonagh, 2020).

Inventing and Murdering the Moron

At the time Nellie F. was admitted to the Royal Albert, the prominent American psychologist Henry H. Goddard was acting as Director of Research at the Vineland Training School for Feeble-Minded Girls and Boys in New Jersey, which enabled him to publish a series of scholarly papers and newspaper articles combining his interests in heredity, intelligence and social hygiene (Trent, 1994). Goddard achieved a considerable degree of fame following the 1912 publication of *The Kallikak Family*, a genealogical study which purported to demonstrate the hereditary of mental deficiency by tracing two branches of one family tree, one apparently untainted by feeblemindedness, the other "a race of defective degenerates" (Goddard, 1912: 103). *The Kallikak Family* established Goddard as one of the world's leading experts on feeblemindedness. Wellcome Collection's copy of this book contains an inscription written by Goddard for G.E. Shuttleworth, Medical Superintendent of the Royal Albert, "in recognition of his great and valuable work for the feebleminded and incidentally his kindness to me personally", again highlighting the power–knowledge network controlling the discourse around mental deficiency. *The Kallikak Family* has since become notorious as pseudoscience if not downright fraudulent, with strong suspicions that large parts of it were fabricated. No such concerns existed to impede its influence at the time, and the book only bolstered Goddard's reputation.

Goddard was also instrumental in popularising the use of intelligence tests, throughout America and abroad. The most commonly used was the Binet–Simon test. As we have seen, the test was in use at the Royal Albert by around 1910. Goddard, like a number of his contemporaries, adapted it for his own purposes. Through manipulating the Binet–Simon test, Goddard created results which apparently confirmed the existence of a new category of feeblemindedness, and he claimed that 2% of all school-age American children belonged to this category. Like a physicist adjusting his optical instruments so as to reveal a suspected yet hitherto invisible property of lightwaves, Goddard's manoeuvre helped bring into being a new "kind" of person, who was held in many ways to resemble a "normal" one but was permanently, unimprovably mentally deficient (Carlson, 2010). Francis Galton was guilty of a similar manipulation, creating dubious composite photographs to support his pseudoscientific phrenological claims (MacDondald, 2017). The moron, the new kind of person Goddard had invented, was taken to represent a particular threat to society because of their potential to pass unnoticed in the general population, combined with their purported propensity for crime and procreation (Trent, 1994). In this way, the moron, a name Goddard derived from the Ancient Greek *moros*, meaning dull, was deliberately invented as a new slot into which people could fall and be counted, and a new way for people to be: of low intelligence and a menace to society.

What is remarkable here is the deliberate creation of a new kind of person. Earlier scientific endeavours aimed at explaining human nature had been restricted to describing, recording and classifying. They were anthropological. Goddard's manoeuvre took the science beyond observation and comparison. In Goddard's hands, the instrument of the Binet–Simon test does not merely capture a certain kind of person who is suspected of being out there, but actively brings them into being (Packer,

2017). The Human – and the less-than-Human – are no longer God's divine creations and subject only to taxonomy. Now, humans not only decide who counts as human, and of what kind, but manipulate and create new kinds of human. The ideal, desirable humans are those much like Goddard and Vitruvian Man: Western, educated, male. The goal becomes to identify as many undesirable humans as possible, and either mould them in the desirable image or, with God-like power, wipe them from the face of the Earth.

All of this follows from the "avalanche of numbers" (Hacking, 2004: 100) which accompanied the Industrial Revolution and its concomitant network of surveillance. We should remember here that the science of statistics was invented in order to control populations, and that the numbers and statistics produced by intelligence tests and their subjects were thus crucial to the eugenics movement (Davis, 1995). The moron is thus born as a new and particularly undesirable type of person, one who represents a particularly menacing threat. It is therefore perhaps not surprising that the invention of the moron was quickly followed by moves to eradicate them and other mental defectives.

Another prominent figure in the eugenics movement at the time was Professor R.J.A. Berry, whose concerns bring us back to Charles Darwin's worries about "Caucasians ceding the Earth to negroes and Aboriginals". Richard James Arthur Berry was born in 1867 in the village of Upholland, Lancashire, about 40 miles from the Royal Albert and well within its catchment area.[3] In 1891, Berry graduated with a degree in medicine from the University of Edinburgh and quickly moved through the ranks of the profession, with posts in Edinburgh and then Melbourne, Australia, where he was appointed Professor of Anatomy at the university, as well as consultant psychiatrist at the nearby children's hospital. He was prominent internationally in the eugenics movement and a particularly influential figure in the study of mental defectiveness. He published extensively in learned journals such as the *Eugenics Review*, gave invited addresses to the British *Eugenics Society* and the Royal Society of Edinburgh, attended lavish Galton Laboratory dinners and so on (Figure 3.4). The menu at the dinner on 23 June 1927 extended to seven courses, champagne and brandy.

This stands in stark contrast to the food offered at places like the Royal Albert. There, inmates were regularly served a dish they nicknamed Blackclock Soup, *blackclock* being a local dialect word for a beetle. Berry's positions afforded him the means to conduct extensive investigations in his own laboratory. His interests revolved around three interrelated topics: cranial anatomy, physical anthropology and mental defectiveness in children. He was aiming to prove suspected links between skull size and intelligence, as evident in the diagnoses of microcephalic idiocy discussed above. Berry's studies of comparative anatomy

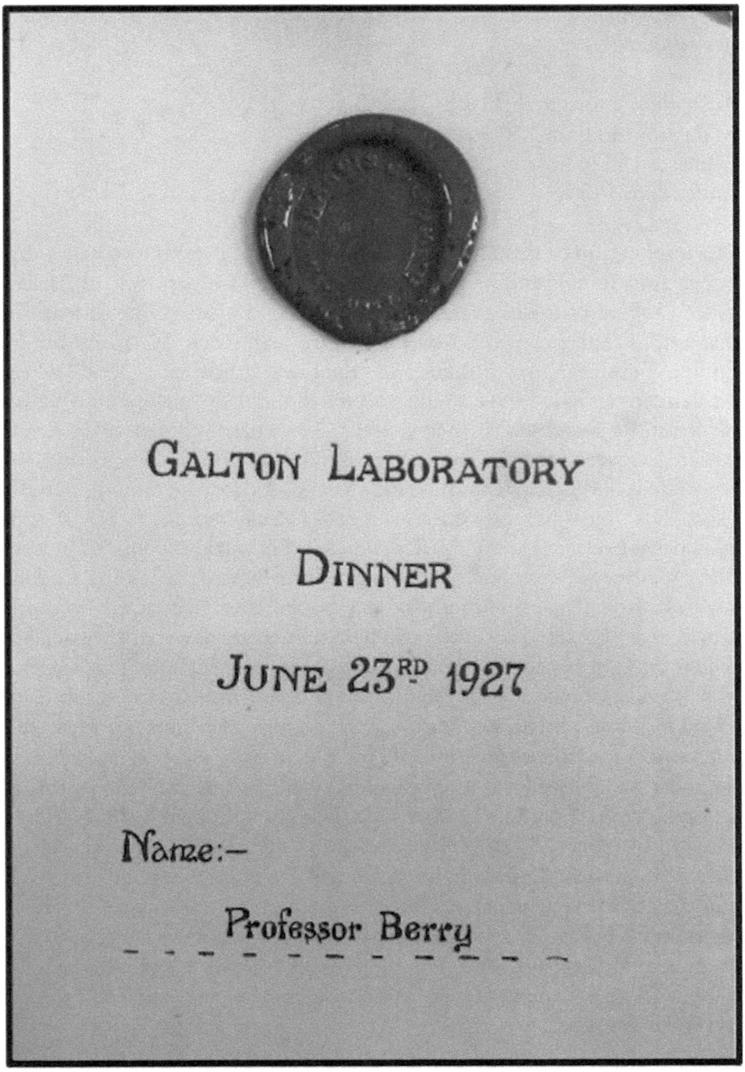

Figure 3.4 Prof Berry's invitation to a Galton Laboratory dinner.

were done on "mentally defective" children, convicted criminals and Aboriginal Australians and Tasmanians. Put simply, he believed that bigger skulls equalled bigger brains and therefore higher intelligence. In one study he conducted by measuring skull volumes to deduce the brain weights of different races of people, he arrived at the following results, which were shared both at public lectures and in Melbourne newspapers:

Australian aboriginal: 1189g
Malay and Indian: 1266g
Chinese: 1332g
Caucasian: 1335g

The implication of this and other similar work of Berry's was that antipodean Aboriginals and people he termed Negroes (i.e. people of African descent) were of lower average intelligence and more prone to learning disabilities than people of Asian and European stock. He made similar findings in relation to criminals and "the lower grades of society", whom he claimed tended to have smaller brains than those "occupying a higher place on the social scale" (Berry, 1912: 10). Forty years after his death, it was discovered that he had collected not only bones from around 400 Aboriginal bodies, by what has since been called grave-robbing, but also brains, also by apparently dubious means (MacDondald, 2017). Despite considerable ethical and empirical flaws in his work, during his lifetime Berry's influence was considerable, and not limited to fellow academics and medical men. He published a book, *Your Brain and Its Story,* aimed at a general audience, as well as numerous newspaper articles in which he used his research findings to argue stridently for the segregation, sterilisation and extermination of people with learning disabilities, all underpinned by an explicitly racist ideology. Perhaps the most succinct and powerful exposition of this ideology – and probably one of the most widely read – is a newspaper article written by Berry, afforded a double-page spread in Melbourne's *The Herald* when published on 3 May 1924 (Berry, 1924). The article was called "The Problem of the Unfit". In person, Berry was forthright, to the point where he ultimately made such powerful enemies in Melbourne that he left Australia, returning to finish his career at Stoke Park Colony for Mentally Defective Children, near Bristol, England. His forceful personality is certainly evident in both the tenor and content of the arguments he makes in *The Problem of the Unfit* and elsewhere.

Berry begins the article by justifying the sorting and classifying of individuals according to perceived intellectual ability in the same manner as boxers are classified by weight, and then laments the ineducability of morons, imbeciles and idiots. He contends that morons, imbeciles and idiots are more like beasts than humans because of their inability to control their lustful and criminal appetites, and that this makes them subhumans outside the scope of the law: "Laws are made by normal people for normal people, but it is quite impossible to teach this elementary fact to the more poorly developed grades of mankind". In the peroration, Berry goes beyond even animalisation, likening people with learning disabilities to both a cloud of toxic gas and prolific nuisance plants, which ought to be eradicated in order to prevent them from corrupting the normal population. The kind of language prominent figures in the eugenics movement like Berry, Goddard and the Huxley[4] brothers used has led them to being considered "pioneer environmentalists" (Linett, 2023: 488), albeit with a very different philosophy to today's ecologically aware citizens. Rather, they were seeking to eliminate parasites – disabled people – from the eugenic tree. They did not see people and planet existing in a symbiotic relationship but as "tapeworm and infested dog, of fungus and blighted potato" (Linett, 2023).

Berry goes on to advocate for enhanced legislation, the establishing of more research laboratories and the foundation of "special village communities", elsewhere known as colonies, "to which the less fit could be removed". Yet even segregation and isolation are not sufficient, in Berry's estimation, to solve the problem of what he calls elsewhere "the festering human refuse heap". He calls for sterilisation and extermination: "Harsh though it may sound, there are still others who would be happier in a lethal chamber or allowed to pass through life in a completely sterile condition". Berry concludes with a rather desperate call for government intervention, echoing Darwin's claim that no man would "allow his worst animals to breed":

> Punch's celebrated advice to those about to marry might be extended to read, don't marry a moron, and don't mistake a disease for a man, for even the Greeks knew that the "gods visit the sins of the fathers upon the children". Even enlightened America, bulging with dollars, is said to spend 500 million dollars more on its human failures than on developing its human assets. What gardener develops his weeds at the expense of his plants? What cattle-breeder rears his animals from degenerate stock? Surely a human soul is worth more than a weed or a mongrel. Where, then, is the politician with the necessary vision to see that this bolstering up of the unfit at the expense of the fit is the worst form of national gambling, inasmuch as it means the State is perpetually the wrong horse?

It is difficult to imagine who might be happier inside a lethal gas chamber than outside it, but eugenics was a mainstream politico-scientific movement in the early 20th century, and similar calls were being sounded around the globe. It would take the abomination of the World War II Nazi Aktion T4 programme for eugenics to lose its respectability and mainstream support, even if it was merely driven underground rather than being completely abandoned as a philosophy and an endeavour. What Berry's invective reveals, in its exemplification of eugenic discourse, is the paradox lying at the heart of the appeal to rationalism. Berry and others like him might strive to present their arguments as dispassionate logic – Caucasian skulls are demonstrably larger and so must house bigger, better brains – but it is difficult to imagine a more nakedly fearful and emotive plea than the one Berry makes in *The Problem of the Unfit*. This is an illustration not only of the myth of the disinterested scientist, but of the impossibility of attaining a rational ideal. We cannot separate our thinking from our emotions, however much some people might try to pretend otherwise.

Conclusion

What we have witnessed in this chapter is a shift, over the span of a few decades, in the character of what it meant to be human. Over this same period, there was a concomitant shift in cultural responses to what we now call learning disability. What remained – and remains – constant is that learning disability figures prominently in conceptualisations of what it means to be human. When human qualities of kindness, pity and charity are valorised, idiots and imbeciles become targets for endeavours which seek to protect and help them. Such ideals are represented in, for example, the lines from *God Help the Imbecile* quoted in the Royal Albert yearbook. When qualities of moral rectitude and fitness to work and to propagate healthy bloodlines are valorised, idiots, imbeciles and the newly invented morons become targets for endeavours which seek to quarantine and even eliminate them. Such endeavours are represented here in the examples of Nelly F and Antonia Grandoni. In this sense, learning disability acts as kind of mirror for what it means to be human. Learning disability mirrors the ambitions and prejudices of the time, whether those are to save or to destroy. This mirror acts in complex ways. It does not merely reflect; it refracts and distorts. The unsettling qualities of the mirror are something Foucault examined in his consideration of heterotopias, or "Other spaces". His description of heterotopias evokes worlds within worlds, emplacements which are simultaneously real and unreal, reflecting, refracting and disrupting other spaces. Thus, in the mirror, we apprehend an illusory virtual space generated by the physical reality of the mirror's surface, yet which we cannot actually inhabit (Foucault and Miskowiec, 1986: 4):

> The mirror functions as a heterotopia in this respect: it makes this place that I occupy at the moment when I look at myself in the glass at once absolutely real, connected with all the space that surrounds it, and absolutely unreal, since in order to be perceived it has to pass through this virtual point which is over there.

Mirrors thus simultaneously and paradoxically affirm and distort our sense of reality. Licia Carlson has elucidated the complex ways in which learning disability performs the mirror function in relation to humanity (Carlson, 2010). Although the mirror might prompt self-examination, the surface of the mirror and the distortions it produces serve to keep people with learning disabilities "over there" in the illusory ground created by the mirror. The mirror maintains the boundary between "the Other" – people with learning disabilities – and Us – people without (Altermark, 2018). We can never step through the mirror.

Much effort is expended in maintaining and policing this boundary. So much effort, in fact, that we go so far as to invent new kinds of human so that we can deny them their humanity. This in itself marks a shift in how the human is conceptualised; we are no longer simply divine creations but can be – and I use this phrase judiciously – man-made. This ability to create signifies immense power. With power comes the ability to direct and control. This brings us to the binary considered in Chapter 4: Controlled / Abandoned.

Notes

1 Equivalent to £125,000 today.
2 It is not clear why Nellie was admitted to an asylum rather than a school for deaf. It is possible that such a school would not have accepted her. It is also possible that a place practising physiological methods would be considered suitable, because they were originally devised for teaching people with sensory impairments.
3 Although the Lancashire County Archives hold a Berry collection as well as the Royal Albert's records, there is no record of him working there.
4 Julian and Aldous Huxley were influential eugenicists. Aldous is perhaps best known now as the author of the ableist science fiction novel *Brave New World*. Julian was a biologist. An excellent if horrifying exposition of his beliefs is available through the short 1937 film *Heredity in Man*, which is free to view via the British Film Institute website www.bfi.org.uk.

References

Alston, J. (1992) *The Royal Albert: Chronicles of an Era*. Lancaster: Centre for North-West Regional Studies, University of Lancaster.
Altermark, N. (2018) *Citizenship Inclusion and Intellectual Disability: Biopolitics Post-Institutionalisation*. Abingdon, Oxon and New York: Routledge (Routledge Advances in Disability Studies).
Ball, S.J. (2012) *Foucault, Power, and Education*. Abingdon, Oxon: Routledge. Available at: https://doi.org/10.4324/9780203078662.

Barden, O. *et al.* (2022) 'Antonia's Story: Bringing the Past into the Future', *British Journal of Learning Disabilities*, 50(2), pp. 258–269. Available at: https://doi.org/10.1111/bld.12447.

Berry, R.J.A. (1912) 'Criminals and Brains: A Professor's Deductions', *Melbourne Argus*, 6 November, p. 10.

Berry, R.J.A. (1924) 'The Problem of the Unfit', *The Herald*, 5 March, pp. 10–11.

Campbell, T. (2013) *Dyslexia: The Government of Reading*. London: Palgrave Macmillan.

Carlson, L. (2010) *The Faces of Intellectual Disability Philosophical Reflections*. Bloomington, IN: Indiana University Press.

Davis, L.J. (1995) *Enforcing Normalcy: Disability, Deafness and the Body*. New York: Verso.

Digby, A. (1996) 'Contexts and Perspectives', in *From Idiocy to Mental Deficiency: Historical Perspectives on People with Learning Difficulties*. Routledge, pp. 1–21.

Foucault, M. and Miskowiec, J. (1986) 'Of Other Spaces', *Diacritics*, 16(1), pp. 22–27. Available at: https://doi.org/10.2307/464648.

Gelb, S.A. (2008) 'Darwin's Use of Intellectual Disability in the Descent of Man', *Disability Studies Quarterly*, 28(2). Available at: https://doi.org/10.18061/dsq.v28i2.96.

Goddard, H.H. (1912) *The Kallikak Family: A Study in the Heredity of Feeble-Mindedness*. New York: Macmillan. Available at: https://archive.org/details/kallikakfamilyst00godd/page/n1/mode/2up.

Hacking, I. (2004) *Historical Ontology*. Cambridge, MA: Harvard University Press.

Ireland, W.W. (1877) *On Idiocy and Imbecility*. London: J.A. Churchill.

Jarrett, S. (2020) *Those They Called Idiots. The idea of the disabled mind from 1700 to the present day*. London: Reaktion Books.

Linett, M. (2023) 'Mind the Gap', *Journal of Literary & Cultural Disability Studies*, 17(4), pp. 435–451. Available at: https://doi.org/10.3828/jlcds.2023.33.

MacDondald, H. (2017) 'Richard Berry's Disgrace', *Overland Literary Journal*. Available at: https://overland.org.au/previous-issues/issue-227/feature-helen-macdonald/ (Accessed: 25 October 2024).

McDermott, R., Goldman, S. and Varenne, H. (2006) 'The Cultural Work of Learning Disabilities', *Educational Researcher*, 35(6), pp. 12–17. Available at: https://doi.org/10.3102/0013189X035006012.

McDonagh, P. (2020) 'Learning Difficulties: The Transformation of "Idiocy" in the Nineteenth Century', in J.L. Huff and M. Stoddard Holmes (eds) *A Cultural History of Disability in the Long Nineteenth Century*. London: Bloomsbury Publishing, pp. 129–147.

Packer, M.J. (2017) *The Science of Qualitative Research*. 2nd edn. Cambridge: Cambridge University Press. Available at: https://doi.org/10.1017/9781108264907.

Royal Commission on the Care and Control of the Feeble-Minded (1908) *Report of the Royal Commission on the Care and Control of the Feeble-Minded*. London: HMSO, Royal Commission on the Care and Control of the Feeble-Minded.

Seguin, E. (1866) *Idiocy: And Its Treatment by the Physiological Method*. New York: William Wood & Co.

Simpson, M.K. (2018) *Modernity and the Appearance of Idiocy: Intellectual Disability as a Regime of Truth*. New York and Lampeter: Edwin Mellen Press.

Smith, D.J. (1999) 'Darwin's Last Child: Mental Retardation and the Need for a Romantic Science', *Mental Retardation*, 37(6), pp. 504–506. Available at: https://doi.org/10.1352/0047-6765(1999)037<0504:DLCMRA>2.0.CO;2.

Snyder, S.L. and Mitchell, D.T. (2006) *Cultural Locations of Disability*. Chicago: Chicago University Press.

Stiker, H.-J. (1999) *A History of Disability*. Ann Arbor: University of Michigan Press.

Trent, J.W. (1994) *Inventing the Feeble Mind: A History of Mental Retardation in the United States*. Berkeley: University of California Press.

4 Controlled *and* Abandoned

Introduction

The paradox explored in this chapter is how people with learning disabilities are simultaneously controlled and abandoned, both within and beyond the walls of the institution. Picking up from where Chapter 3 left off, it initially charts the move away from overtly eugenic policy and practices towards deinstitutionalisation, normalisation and care in the community. These postwar decades seemed to offer some hope of emancipation, and some significant gains were indeed made in terms of learning-disabled people's inclusion in society. Yet what was presented as care was in fact no more than another form of control: assessing, diagnosing, classifying, sorting and segregating. Then, the veneer of progress quickly cracked in the early decades of the 21st century, and its shaky foundations were exposed. The twin shocks of austerity and the global COVID-19 pandemic again highlighted the power of dehumanising metanarrative: people with learning disabilities were less worthy than others, more vulnerable and required more control. Perversely, measures taken supposedly to care for and control people with learning disabilities actually resulted in them being abandoned, whether inside a cell within the archipelago of control, or in a bedroom in their own home. How this can be so is examined in the latter part of the chapter. What the chapter illustrates is that despite the latter-day rhetoric of inclusion, our fundamental regard for people with learning disabilities has, in the main, changed very little.

Controlling Care

Up until the end of World War II, eugenics was a mainstream politico-scientific project, with widespread support. It was not only perpetrated by Hitler's Nazis; Winston Churchill, for example, is known to have believed in the kind of racial hierarchies Darwin and Berry's work helped to construct and promote, and also advocated for eugenics.

DOI: 10.4324/9781003411925-4

Similarly, the mayors of the English cities of Portsmouth and Nottingham both advocated extermination of the feebleminded. The Nottingham Evening Post of 8 June 1909 reported the Mayor of Portsmouth as saying that "It is possible to submit these idiots to a painless death and release them from the purgatory of non-intelligence" (Stewart, 2017). In the United States, the Eugenics Records Office at Cold Spring Harbor Laboratory in New York, then under the directorship of Charles Davenport and known as the Carnegie Institution of Washington, established and maintained connections with the German racial hygiene movement throughout the 1920s and 1930s. However, as the world recoiled from World War II and the Nazi regime, and eugenics lost respectability, there appeared to be something of a softening of attitudes towards people with learning disabilities. At this time, Lord Richard Cavendish was Chairman of the Central Committee, which was the top administrative layer for asylums in the United Kingdom until they were incorporated into the National Health Service. In 1940, he made the following statement in prestigious British medical journal *The Lancet:*

> The social attitude of most people towards the fate of mentally defective people strikes me nowadays as odd. At one time I shared their opinion and advocated euthanasia was the best: but that was before I had much to do with mentally defective patients. Even after a month or two in the wards I was pretty cocksure – but little by little I found I was wrong. The easy superiority of the eugenicist deserted me, for I found that I was dealing, not with regrettable accidents, but with people, and uncommonly nice people at that.
>
> After five years of their society, and the time has been spent among low-grade defectives, idiots and imbeciles, I know that if someone presented me with a fine new lethal chamber and authority to use it, I should have extreme difficulty in choosing even one victim. On what grounds ought the choice to be made? Mere lack of intelligence seems a dangerous standard. Many high-grade defectives . . . would not be noticeably deficient if placed among simple or savage people: they would do pretty well. It seems unreasonable to say that if they had been born scions of a race of savages they would be fit to survive, but that having cropped up in a civilized country they merit death. Most of them are kindly, innocent, easily contented, easily amused and willing to work endlessly at a dull job without losing interest . . . on the whole they are good citizens.
>
> (Cavendish, 1940; cited in Alston, 1992: 78)

In contrast to prior widespread support of euthanasia, here was an outright rejection. Yet despite the apparent sympathy, a racialised dehumanising attitude can readily be discerned in Cavendish's appreciation of how *uncommonly nice* the *defectives* are, despite being somewhat akin to *savages* or *simple people* who, although they are *good citizens*, somehow do not belong in *civilized society*. These statements echo the sentiments Mary Dendy, who was prominent in the study and education of the feebleminded in the UK, had expressed almost 30 years earlier in an appendix to the 1911 *Report of the Royal Commission on the Care and Control of the Feeble-Minded*:

> Fortunately, the feebleminded are much more easily made happy than sane persons . . . though no normal man or woman could live a happy life in the restricted conditions which ought to be provided for the weak in intellect, it is perfectly easy to make the majority of the weak-minded happy without ever letting them see anything of the outside world. It is indeed essential to their happiness that they should be so secluded; there is probably no more miserable being on earth than the weak-minded person who is at large.
>
> (Royal Commission on the Care and Control of the Feeble-Minded, 1908: 105)

Extermination might now appear to be off the agenda, yet the metanarrative of learning disability was still operating. People with learning disabilities were still regarded as vulnerable, unworthy of full personhood and requiring control (Barden and Walden, 2021). This was evident in their continued ostracisation within the archipelago of control that had established itself across the globe in the period after the mid-19th century. In the decades after World War II, there was a gradual transition away from geographical segregation and towards deinstitutionalisation. "Care in the community" policies and programmes which seemed to promise greater integration and inclusion slowly came to the fore.

Yet dehumanising attitudes and practices were still commonplace. In asylums, daily disciplinary routines and practices were often aligned more closely with the prison or even the farmyard than the hospital or school. Take the example of bathing: former residents and staff of the Royal Albert Asylum in Lancaster have, in oral history interviews, recalled the routines for bathing that were in operation from the 1920s right up until the 1980s. Inmates were entitled to two baths per week. Baths were communal, with up to six people sharing a bath at any one time. The baths were tepid at best, with one of the 12 rules for bathing stipulating a maximum temperature of 98°F / 37°C (i.e. blood temperature). One former nurse likened the baths to a sheep dip. A bath in cold, dirty water at the Royal Albert does not sounds like an appealing prospect for anyone even at the best of times, yet residents recalled one of their contemporaries having his jaw broken by a punch from a member of staff for attempting to resist a bath (Unlocking the Past, 2010b, 2010a).

Of course, bathing routines were not the only evidence of dehumanising attitudes towards institution residents; clothing was also communal and had to be taken from pre-prepared bundles, and there was the infamous Blackclock (beetle) Soup. Inmates could be sent to a punishment ward for weeks for writing letters to boyfriends or girlfriends. They might be flogged simply for trying to move seats in the dining hall. Even when they were discharged, residents had to exit via a side-door; only staff were permitted to use the main entrance. Many such institutions had burial grounds, yet graves were marked with copper tags fastened to nearby trees rather than with headstones: the metanarrative continued to dehumanise people even after they had died (Barden, 2020a).

On 5 July 1948, the Royal Albert was, like other such UK institutions, absorbed into newly formed National Health Service (NHS). This meant more money was available since funding now came from Central Government rather than solicited subscriptions, which were unreliable and usually insufficient sources of funding. As a result, there were improvements in things like clothing, furnishings and décor. Large institutions like the Royal Albert already resembled hospitals in many ways, having facilities including operating theatres, X-ray rooms, sick bays, pathology laboratories and mortuaries (Hindmarch, 1992). Being subsumed into the NHS meant that the character of such institutions changed, and therefore so did the role of patients. Hitherto, it had been common in institutions in both the United Kingdom and the United States for patients to be given work to do. This included domestic work such as cleaning, baking and laundry duties, crafts including basket-weaving, shoemaking and toolmaking and so on, as well as agricultural labour. It was also commonplace for so-called high-grade residents to be given work caring for their low-grade fellows (Trent, 1994; Wright and Digby, 1996). Ostensibly, this work was designed to help prepare residents for the outside world, and this is how it was promoted by institutional agents. These kinds of work are exactly the sorts of "dull jobs" that were deemed suitable for keeping such "uncommonly nice, easily contented" people occupied, and had the added advantage of contributing to institutional self-sufficiency. Keeping costs down by exploiting people for free or very cheap labour was certainly useful when many institutions were in frequent financial straits. This exploitation was defended on the grounds that it gave residents some sense of purpose and dignity – overlooking the fact that residents only needed a sense of dignity and purpose restored to their lives because actions motivated by the metanarrative of learning disability had resulted in their removal.

Under the new regime, many of the jobs people with learning disabilities had been doing were taken over by NHS staff, leaving residents with little to occupy themselves. As a result, the purpose of the institutions like the Royal Albert became less and less about education and training and more about custodial care. They were run in a similar fashion to acute hospitals despite being long-stay residential sites. Nevertheless, greater recognition of patients' humanity and domestic and social requirements began to develop through the 1950s and 1960s; in a foreshadowing of normalisation policies of the 1970s, discipline and sexual segregation was relaxed, and parole was introduced, whereby patients were permitted to make unaccompanied visits into the local town and area.

A number of additional factors then contributed to the shift towards care in the community, again shaped by medical, political, economic and philosophical discourses. Several institutional scandals, whereby the maltreatment of residents was brought to the public's attention, surfaced in the 1960s, although these were attributed to lack of funding and overcrowding rather than disablist attitudes. Meanwhile, an "explosion" (Alston, 1992: 91) of research into what was now called "mental handicap" in the UK was revealing that the learning abilities of people held in such institutions had been hugely underestimated and their potential was much greater than had previously been thought. At the same time, there was a growing recognition of human rights, with, for example, Erving Goffman's work on stigma and total institutions prompting questioning of whether institutions could provide an environment which would nurture rather than stifle human beings. In the UK, two key pieces of legislation came into force. The 1959/60 Mental Health Acts (England and Wales/Scotland respectively) repealed the Mental Deficiency Acts, espousing community care but providing little funding. The 1971 White Paper *Better Services for the Mentally Handicapped* (Department of Health and Social Security / Welsh Office, 1971) also advocated care in the community.

Better Services augured a sea change in Government policy on provision for people with – what were now starting to be called – learning disabilities. This change in policy reflected a change in philosophy, which had roots in Scandinavian legislation and normalisation theory (Wolfensberger, 1972; Nirje, 1982) and was gaining ground in the United States and Britain. In this philosophy, people with learning disabilities were explicitly recognised as having the same human rights as other citizens. Adherents advocated that disabled people should participate in society and live lives that were as similar as possible to those of non-disabled people, whilst recognising that although disabled people and their families would share some needs with other families, they would also be likely to have specific or individual support requirements in order to be able to live and participate in regular communities. The model of care changed from segregation in institutions which purported to protect patients from the outside world – but whose primary function was instead to protect the outside world from the unfit – to community care. However, like most others, the UK Government did not make any money available with which to implement either the closure of hospitals or the resettlement of residents; hospitals had to use whatever funds were made available through declining patient numbers and resulting cost reductions. The multi-agency support services which replaced the institutions were also poorly resourced. This failure to adequately fund the new policy – that is, to fund the lives of people with learning disabilities – indicates the strength of the prejudicial attitudes that were still prevalent. Many people with learning disabilities were no longer necessarily enclosed by their immediate physical environment, within the panoptic architecture of asylums, colonies and hospitals – although the archipelago of confinement continued to flourish and morph, as we shall see in the next section – but nevertheless were still trapped within a metanarrative that characterised them as unworthy. Initially, the professions and institutions of confinement had attempted to assume authority over the problem of the unfit by relocating and segregating stigmatised individuals and assuring the public that the problem was under control. Now, with normalisation and then community care, rather than being directly controlled through institutionalisation and associated practices, many people with learning disabilities were simply being abandoned. Paradoxical as it may seem, people could be – and still are – abandoned *within* institutions and not just outside of them.

The 21st-Century Archipelago of Control

The move to care in the community and supported or independent living witnessed in the latter part of the 20th century was in part a reaction to the scandalous abuse and neglect evident in many institutions, initially exposed in the 1950s and 1960s, and in part due to growing recognition of disabled people's human rights and capabilities. In theory, it should have led to a more humane, civilised and socially integrated way of life for people labelled with learning disabilities. The UK Government's 2001 White Paper *Valuing People* (Department of Health, 2001), for instance, predicted that by 2004 almost all learning-disabled people would be living essentially ordinary lives in ordinary homes alongside their fellow non-disabled citizens, albeit with the necessary supports. However, much evidence seems to suggest that rather than these policies and practices leading to the emancipation of people labelled with learning disabilities, all that has happened is a reconfiguration of power relations, "one that is entirely in keeping with the modern drive to greater efficiency" (Drinkwater, 2015: 230). Those imagined ordinary lives failed to materialise, and many people with learning disabilities continued – and continue – to reside in the archipelago of control. For example, both Niklas Altermark and Chris Drinkwater have documented the ways in which neoliberal governmentality operates in group homes for people with learning disabilities, in Sweden and the UK, respectively (Altermark, 2018; Drinkwater, 2015). Across the globe, little emancipatory progress has been made in spite of inclusive rhetoric and legislation like the United Nations Convention on the Rights of Persons with Disabilities (Walmsley and Jarrett, 2021). This section highlights the ways people both within and outside the archipelago have frequently been abandoned by the societies that purported to value, support and include them.

Abandoned Inside

Nowadays, the archipelago of control includes a wide variety of penal, medical and educational institutions such as immigration detention centres, prisons, group homes, special schools, secure hospitals and youth detention centres. Many people with learning disabilities, especially those who are deemed to have the most "complex needs" or "challenging behaviours", are permanently warehoused in these institutions. Often, the neoliberal imperative to maximise corporate profits reciprocally drives dehumanising attitudes and practices, resulting in people being abandoned within the very institutions – and by the very people – who are supposed to care for them. This is evident in the litany of scandals reported in recent years.

In 2011, the BBC's investigative current affairs programme *Panorama* exposed systematic abuse and neglect of people with learning disabilities at the Winterbourne View Hospital in Gloucestershire, England. This was the kind of abuse that was supposedly consigned to history with the demise of the asylums. Physical restraint was commonplace and the reporter witnessed many incidences of hitting, slapping, bullying, mockery, often seemingly for the staff's own amusement. In an echo of the Royal Albert's bathing regimes, one inmate was subjected to cold showers, left lying on the ground in wet clothes in near-freezing temperatures, and had mouthwash repeatedly poured into her eyes (Casey, 2011). In another distressing echo of the Royal Albert, a young man named Conor Sparrowhawk (nicknamed Laughing Boy), drowned in the bath because of neglect in the NHS residential unit that was supposed to be caring for him (Inquest.org.uk, 2015). Despite convictions in the Winterbourne View case, a Government inquiry, ensuing publication of a Programme of Action, the Justice for LB campaign (Ryan, 2017), we are continually presented with evidence of the segregation, maltreatment and exploitation of people labelled with learning disabilities. Institutional scandals are still reported regularly. Some evidence suggests that, in the UK, someone with a learning disability is subjected to inhumane treatment every 12 minutes within an institution that is purportedly caring for them (Mencap, 2021). As just one example: in June 2017, 13 directors, managers and carers from Atlas Project Team were convicted over abuse of adults with learning disabilities at two residential homes in Devon, both isolated farmhouses. Atlas Project Team claimed to provide specialist care for learning-disabled people, at a reported cost of up to £4,000 per week per person. One resident had been moved from Winterbourne View after its closure. As at Winterbourne View, and indeed the Royal Albert, residents were punished for trivial transgressions, including staring at a staff member, facial twitches or asking questions repeatedly. Sometimes residents were punished by being denied food, drink, fun activities and visits. They were confined in bare seclusion rooms for hours and sometimes overnight, on occasions wetting or soiling themselves because there were no bathroom facilities. One resident described his experiences so:

> It was a room that was disgusting and cold. At night the door was locked. It had a CCTV camera, a smoke detector and a punctured mattress – it was an airbed but it had a puncture in. It was cold, damp. If you wanted to go to the toilet, there was no toilet in there. There was a window but it was locked. No curtains. They made the room as bad as possible and as uncomfortable as possible. . . . It made me feel terrible in a way . . . an animal, basically.
>
> (Morris, 2017: np)

One of those convicted was Paul Hewitt, the company founder. He was a well-known figure in mental health circles in the UK, having helped formulate national policy on caring for people with learning disabilities in the community. He told the court he did not know what was going on. This claim is itself telling. It highlights the abandonment of people with learning disabilities within the institutions, and by the people, charged with caring for them. Either Hewitt knew what was going on and chose not to intervene, or he really did not know, a situation which would have helped the abuse to continue. Whether by accident or design, the people in these two homes were abandoned to abject lives. The intention here is not to single out one person, but to highlight one illustrative case. The scenario reported here is by no means unique to the UK. Across the archipelago in Australia, for example, the abuse of Dylan Voller and other children at a youth detention centre in the Northern Territory was exposed on national television (McCausland and Baldry, 2017). Voller, a 16-year old disabled Aboriginal with a history of early trauma, was filmed hooded and strapped to a chair. Dylan was being punished for spitting at staff, chewing his mattress and making a mess with toilet paper. His mother reported that he had been kept in isolation for 200 days at a time: another example of abandonment. Voller's case again illustrates how moves to control and "care for" people with learning disabilities in fact result in their being abandoned. Even some school classrooms have been likened to prison cells, with children being left sat alone in piles of vomit, leading some to self-harm for prolonged periods (Challenging Behaviour Foundation, 2024). Even as I write this, the BBC are reporting on a learning-disabled autistic women, Kasibba (a pseudonym), who was wrongly locked up in a secure hospital for 45 years, 25 of which were in long-term segregation, starting when she was 7 years old. It is believed she arrived in the UK having been trafficked from Sierra Leone. She often spent over 23 hours a day locked in her room. Staff nicknamed her the "eye-gouger" and this sobriquet was used to help justify her treatment. Investigations revealed that she had once accidentally scratched another patient's eye in a moment of distressed confusion when a fire alarm had been set off. People who have since come to know Kasibba describe her as a beautiful human being with a wonderful sense of humour, fond of hugging: anything but an eye-gouger (Atkinson and Robinson, 2025)

What these cases unequivocally show us is that people labelled with learning disabilities are routinely being subjected to oppressive, inhumane and degrading treatment. Horrifying as some of their acts might be, it is imperative to not simply blame the staff in these institutions for this set of circumstances. Interlocking discourses of policy, legislation, corporate strategy, vulnerability and challenging behaviour lead those workers, inexorably, into conceptualising the people in their care as risks to be managed. People labelled with learning disabilities are constituted as risks to the wider society, to themselves, to staff and to profits. This results in restrictive practices which have legislative approval only as measures of last resort becoming normalised and commonplace (Care Quality Commission, 2020). Such practices include the administration of drugs approved for short-term use for years at a time, in addition to seclusion, "mechanical restraints" like harnesses, "aversive technologies" such as inflicting pain, electric shocks and the forced inhalation of ammonia (Adams and Erevelles, 2017), as well as the kinds of "physical restraint" performed on Dylan Voller. In the UK, the Care Quality Commission (CQC) – the independent regulator of health and adult social care in England – recently quoted one person who had been subjected to such frequent restraints as saying: "I feel absolutely f***ing sh*t about being restrained. It makes me feel . . . dehumanised. I don't feel like a real human being" (Care Quality Commission, 2020: 20).

A paradox workers face is that although neoliberalism aims to produce "prudent workers with enhanced responsibility", it also provides "the framework and mechanisms necessary to blame, penalize and ultimately remove from the workforce" anybody who is deemed to be acting irresponsibly, in order that organisational reputation and profit are not put at risk (Spivakovsky, 2017: 378). Acting irresponsibly includes workers putting their own health and safety at risk. In an institution where violence, under the pervasive euphemism of challenging behaviour, is perceived to be a constant threat, workers respond to this threat to their health and safety – and hence their continued employment – by enacting restrictive practices as a matter of course, all in the name of managing risk. One is on record as saying:

> The problem is that a lot of this stuff makes it easier for workers, and sometimes safer for workers – keeping people under control – and I think that means that things like workplace health and safety can be used as a technique for maintaining coercion and control.
>
> (Spivakovsky, 2017)

My point here is that overworked, poorly paid and poorly trained employees as well as residents find themselves constrained by a discursive regime of truth (Foucault, 1980; Simpson, 2018), or metanarrative, which constructs people with learning disabilities as risky Others. Power is exerted through the relationships between these two groups, with the organising concept of *learning disability* constituting workers as moral agents – protecting everyone from risk, and hence harm – whose apparent professional freedom to act is in fact confined within the very limited space of possibilities afforded by current and historical political, legal, economic and medical discourses. Of course, the prevailing politico-economic discourse of our times in many parts of the globe is neoliberalism. With its twin ideals of maximising corporate profits and minimising State involvement, neoliberalism has contributed immeasurably to the abandoning of people with learning disabilities within institutions.

The marketisation of provision for and "care" of people with learning disabilities has also created a trade in people (Brown *et al.*, 2017) who are treated as though they were livestock (Taylor, 2011). People in long-term segregation in the UK are moved, on average, between three institutions in five years. This market generates huge revenues in the UK and globally: the UK spends around £0.5 billion every year keeping about 2000 people labelled with learning disabilities in hospitals (around 200 of whom are children) with just over half of those beds provided by the private sector rather than the National Health Service. The number of inpatients is still around 2000 despite the Government launching the Transforming Care programme and the Building the Right Support national plan in 2015, which committed to closing 35–50% inpatient beds by March 2019 and supporting people to return home. In fact, in addition to the number of inpatients remaining above 2,000, the quality of provision seems to have deteriorated. In 2022, the Care

Quality Commission conducted 150 unannounced inspections of NHS and private hospitals and care homes for people with learning disabilities. Nearly half of the institutions inspected did not meet national standards, and the CQC said that staff still needed to be given appropriate training in restraint techniques (Care Quality Commission, 2022).

Fifteen years ago, only one in five beds in such places were in the private sector, meaning there has been significant growth in private sector provision, and hence money going to the private sector, to the point where the private sector now plays the greater role. A learning-disabled person who has been in a UK hospital for five years will generate on average over £1 million in income for an independent sector organisation, although significantly higher levels of income are possible. Private providers are tending to locate their institutions where operating costs are lower, as indicated by real estate prices. Efficiency and profit thus appear to take precedence over care, support and education. This leads to people labelled with learning disabilities being sent to locations far-distant from their families (Care Quality Commission, 2021). Moreover, under the current funding regime, when such a person is registered with a General Practitioner[1] close to the hospital they are now resident in, as is standard practice, the health authority in that area (known as CCG, Clinical Commissioning Group) becomes responsible for the cost of any aftercare, rather than the person's original "home" authority. Inevitably, because these costs are substantial, CCGs are reluctant to meet them, providing further incentive for continued confinement in some cases. In other cases, people are discharged to institutions outside the area, meaning they will have to register with a different GP and hence become another CCG's financial responsibility. These factors mean that people labelled with learning disabilities are being traded like commodities in order to generate profits, as providers make exchanges based on the types of provision they do and don't have. These providers unabashedly use the language of commerce in describing what they do. Here is a quote from a report of the Southampton, Hampshire, Isle of Wight and Portsmouth (SHIP) Transforming Care Partnership, cited in (Brown *et al.*, 2017: 8):

> The SHIP TCP is a nett importer of people with Learning Difficulties . . . plus a nett exporter of inpatients as there are no beds on Portsea Island.

And another, from Northamptonshire:

> Northamptonshire is a County with several large providers and this has created an "importer" concern. . . . St Andrews is a large [independent] provider of services for people with learning disabilities.

> This hospital is in the process of expanding with a new 100 bed service for people with autism which is a significant concern for the CCGs from an economical and value-based perspective.

The cold and calculating language of commerce – of import and exports, of value-based perspectives – exposes the lack of care both *about* and *for* people with learning disabilities. The Clinical Commissioning Group's concern is a detached, disinterested economic one. These quotes illustrate quite baldly an ideology which regards people with learning disabilities as little more than economic units to be summed, sorted and shifted. This narrow and unrelenting focus on monetary matters is nowhere more evident than in our very recent history of austerity, an agenda which led to the abandonment of many people with learning disabilities who live outside of institutions. The prejudice and discrimination they face was magnified first by austerity before swelling and metastasising during the COVID-19 pandemic.

Abandoned Outside

The quality of care people with learning disabilities receive outside of institutions, in the community, is varied and by no means perfect, but does tend to be better than that within them. Many people with learning disabilities are able to live relatively full, autonomous lives, doing the things they like to do. But this position is precarious. Social shockwaves quickly expose the fault lines lurking beneath everyday lives. This is evident in the toll taken by austerity measures in the UK and elsewhere, the impacts of which were amplified by the COVID-19 pandemic. In such times of crisis, people with learning disabilities are amongst the first to be abandoned.

The UK Government instituted its austerity programme in 2010. It tried to justify this programme by arguing that it needed to reduce the public deficit and avoid damaging interest payments on the country's debts, following the global financial crisis of 2008. Although the Government found the money to bail out the banks who had caused the crisis, they claimed not to be able to afford to support citizens rendered destitute by austerity policies (Bates *et al.*, 2017). The UK austerity programme has thus been characterised as "the four D's" (Arrieta, 2022: 239): disinvestment, decentralisation, decollectivisation and disintegration. It involved reducing expenditure on public services (disinvestment); shifting responsibility for delivering services from central to local government (decentralisation); individualising labour relations, for example, by downgrading the power of trade unions (decollectivisation); and the fragmentation and increasing privatisation of services, as discussed in relation to "care" in the previous section of this chapter (disintegration).

Austerity badly affected many people, but poorer and disabled people disproportionately so. People with learning disabilities were amongst the worst affected: it became harder and harder to find work, with Mencap estimating in 2016 that in the UK, only around one in five people with a learning disability had a job (Mencap, 2016). This is around half the rate of employment of other disabled people, and a quarter of the rate of non-disabled people. At the same time, welfare payments were reduced or cut entirely, meaning many were left in poverty; supports and services in and outside the home were also cut, sometimes drastically; increased isolation meant many lacked friends and were lonely, with their quality of life and mental health negatively impacted (Carpenter, 2018). In the middle of all this, Brexit was triggered in 2016, prompting many employees in the health and care sectors to return to their home countries, exacerbating service shortcomings. Related effects were felt by members of their families and support networks. In parallel with paid care workers being trapped by the metanarrative of learning disability, family members and volunteers who stepped in to care as services disappeared or became reactionary and overwhelmed were also abandoned by the State. They were given no money or guidance for doing this work, and many had to leave their normal paid jobs – supposedly the neoliberal *sine qua non* – to take on these caring roles.

The UK was certainly not alone in adopting austerity; it was widespread, especially in Europe. Returning briefly to Sweden as an example – claimant numbers for disability benefits there reduced by two-thirds in the period 2004–2015, thanks mainly to austerity policies (Malli *et al.*, 2018). But both austerity and inequality were particularly vicious in the UK. Government ministers – including Eton and Oxford-educated Prime Minister David Cameron – liked to assert that "we are all in this together" but this lie was exposed time and time again. One memorable example was when Iain Duncan Smith – then Work and Pensions Secretary, responsible for the welfare system – claimed a £39 breakfast on parliamentary expenses: an amount similar to that a disabled person on welfare might have to live on for week. Duncan Smith was also the architect of Housing Benefit reforms which became known popularly as the Bedroom Tax. Under these reforms, implemented in 2013, families had their welfare payments reduced or were forcibly relocated if their accommodation was deemed by officials to be too large (Bray *et al.*, 2024). This led, for instance, to Rob Tomlinson, a man with cerebral palsy, having to be bathed by his parents in a child's paddling pool after the family were evicted from their specially adapted home in Southport, a seaside town north of Liverpool (Liverpool Echo, 2015). Duncan Smith, meanwhile, lived rent-free in a Tudor mansion replete with tennis courts and swimming pool, owned by his wife's aristocratic family (Mudie, 2013).

These inequalities were pernicious and pervasive, and evident in healthcare and education. For example, in 2016, people with learning disabilities were much more likely to have physical or mental health problems than other people, leading to much higher rates of hospital admissions compared with non-disabled people (Bates *et al.*, 2017). Even though people with learning disabilities were more likely to become ill, the quality of care they received was often poor, and they were much more likely to die prematurely than other disabled people and non-disabled people (Heslop, *et al.*, 2013; LeDeR, 2017). Inequalities in education also increased; formal and informal exclusions of children with labels of Special Educational Needs / Disabilities (SEND), particularly those described as having "challenging behaviour", rose at the same time as it became harder to obtain a personalised Education, Health and Care Plan (EHCP), in part because of local Councils' need to reduce expenditure, Central Government having reduced budgets (Gates, 2019): disinvestment, decentralisation, disintegration.

For these reasons, learning-disabled people's experience of austerity has been characterised as essentially one of loss: loss of income; loss in the range and quality of services, supports and activities available; loss of social connections; and ultimately loss of autonomy and dignity (Malli et al., 2018; Forrester-Jones *et al.*, 2021). The loss of dignity resulting from the stripping away of State provisions was compounded by increasingly hostile media reporting of disability and disabled people. As early as 2011, it was noted that there was simultaneously an uptick in the amount of news stories devoted to disability and a shift towards more politicised, hostile tone (Briant *et al.*, 2011). Disabled people were increasingly portrayed as shirkers and scroungers, claiming benefit payments fraudulently. The reality was – and still is – that the amount lost to the Treasury to disability benefit fraud (which tends to be perpetrated by non-disabled people) is negligible. Yet the British public thought that 70% of claims were fraudulent. Underpayment of disability benefits ought to be far greater concern; at the time of writing, this figure stands at £750 million, or 11% of all payments (Committee of Public Accounts, 2025). Nevertheless, the increase in hostile coverage triggered by austerity appeared to coincide with a hardening of public attitudes. Incidences of disability hate crime quickly rose by 18%, to record levels (The Guardian Datablog, 2012). Disability hate crimes and incidents became normalised to the extent that many disabled people came to expect a "drip, drip, nag nag of low-level harassment" (EHRC, quoted in Burch, 2022: 394). Correlation may not be causation, but it is difficult to imagine there was no link between aggressive austerity programmes, spiteful media stories and rising disability hate crime.

The fissures in the social fabric austerity exposed yawned wide open under the pressures of COVID-19. In the preceding years, successive

Learning Disabilities Mortality Review (LeDeR) reports had shown unequivocally that, in the UK, there were substantial inequalities in healthcare for people with learning disabilities, and they were more likely that most die a premature death. This pattern was amplified by the pandemic. In the UK, the Office for National Statistics reported in February 2021 that disabled people were three times as likely as non-disabled people to die from coronavirus. Learning-disabled people's risk of death from COVID-19 in the UK was four times greater than people without. Their mortality rate was higher even when controlling for other characteristics; in other words, they were more likely to die *because* they had a learning disability. Many disabled people who had underlying conditions were more at risk of contracting the virus and of death, and lack of protection measures put them even more at risk. The fact that COVID-19 could present differently in people with learning disabilities was often not taken into account. There were also significant problems with the responsiveness of NHS 111, access to COVID-19 tests and access to specialist learning disability nurses (Care Quality Commission, 2021).

This bleak scenario was aggravated when questionable decision-making was coupled with old age and susceptibility to infection. In the UK, when there was sudden need for NHS beds, Matt Hancock, then Secretary of State for Health and Social Care, mandated that people who may have COVID – whether symptomatic or asymptomatic – could be safely discharged to care homes, unleashing a deathly wave of COVID cases and deaths in disabled older people living in care homes. Cuts were made to social care and it took a very long time for people with learning disabilities to be prioritised in access to vaccinations, despite them being at greater risk of death. Similarly, people with learning disabilities who had COVID-19 encountered what charities described as shocking discrimination when those in hospital were given Do Not Resuscitate orders, without their or their families' knowledge or consent. These examples demonstrate some of the carelessness and poor decision-making which brought into sharp focus contemporary manifestations of a long history of prejudice, discrimination, segregation and oppression. Inclusion London's February 2021 report "Locked Down and Abandoned: Disabled People's Experiences of Covid-19" detailed a range of negative impacts across mental health, employment and finance, social care and support, healthcare and community access. Many such services – day services, education placements, respite care and health services – had no plan for people with learning disabilities during the pandemic. This scenario created significant and widespread distress, not just for people with learning disabilities but also for people in their family and support networks. Post-COVID, many aspects of social life slowly returned to some kind of normal, but this did not mean that the lives and prospects of people with learning disabilities dramatically improved. In the UK, the current Labour Government's stated need to deal with the fiscal black hole it claimed to inherit from an irresponsible preceding Conservative administration has contributed to further cuts to services, whilst inequalities – such as in waiting times for medical treatment – remain (Learning Disability England, 2025; Social Finance, 2025). As Niklas Altermark has argued (Altermark, 2018), this abandonment is itself a form of control. It is a mode of governance which operates through technologies of abnormality and surveillance, through structuring – narrowing – the field of possibilities open to people with learning disabilities, through the propagation and internalisation of ableism, through shaping non-disabled and learning-disabled peoples' perceptions of their place in society.

Conclusion

This chapter has examined the history of learning disability over the last hundred years or so, principally in the UK but with nods to Europe and America. What can we learn about learning disability, and what it means to be human, from this recent history and this history of the present? Perhaps there are two obvious conclusions. I am far from the first to point this out, but one conclusion is that although there may at times be superficial progress towards recognising and appreciating the full humanity of people with learning disabilities, we have not yet eliminated our dehumanising core. Despite the rhetoric of progress, inclusion, community and care, people with learning disabilities are still widely regarded as inferior. Prejudicial, ableist attitudes have resulted, and continue to result in, disablist abandonment both with and beyond the walls of the physical manifestations of the archipelago of confinement. James Trent captured this wonderfully in his introduction to *Inventing the Feeble Mind:*

> From the time people with "the thing", mental retardation, became social problems requiring help and treatment, the contours this requirement have changed, sometimes dramatically, but the contours of our regard for people with mental retardation have not. This or that must be done to and for them; this and that must be learned about them and said about them to ensure progress in treatment technologies, professional influence, institutional funding, or social control.
>
> (Trent, 1994: 6)

The texture of the narrative around learning disability may have softened, from harsh cries for extermination to the feelgood phrasing of inclusion, but the underlying contours of our regard for people labelled with learning disabilities have not changed much. They have not changed because we are enveloped by a powerful metanarrative. This metanarrative characterises people with learning disabilities as less than human, and as requiring control. It privileges psychomedical knowledge and perspectives, and silences emic ways of knowing. Meanwhile, the cultural work that learning disability has done in relation to our understanding of what it means to be human is manifold (McDermott *et al.*, 2006). It includes work to provide Others against which Normals can be defined and measured; work to legitimate professional medical, legal, educational and health power-knowledge regimes; and to provide careers for professionals who "care" for fellow humans labelled as defective or risky, and profits for companies employing those people. This brings us to our second obvious conclusion: that the value of human life is currently often largely perceived in terms of economic value and contribution. People with learning disabilities are less valuable as people – and therefore less human – because they earn less and contribute less to the economy, even as they generate corporate profits when being traded like cattle.

In short, learning disability has worked as an organising concept; one which has radically transformed our sense not only of education and learning, but also of who is or is not deemed entitled to full citizenship and the associated rights, and so who is or is not fully human. And this has undeniably made for rather grim reading and for dire consequences for many people with learning disabilities. However, in the next and final chapter, I turn to a relatively new way of understanding what it means to be human, the philosophy of posthumanism. I believe posthuman offers opportunities for positive and inclusive reframings of both learning disability and of what it means to be human.

Note

1 GP; family physician.

References

Adams, D. and Erevelles, N. (2017) 'Unexpected Spaces of Confinement: Aversive Technologies, Intellectual Disability, and "Bare Life"', *Punishment & Society*, 19(3), pp. 348–365. Available at: https://doi.org/10.1177/1462474517705147.

Alston, J. (1992) *The Royal Albert: Chronicles of an Era.* Lancaster: Centre for North-West Regional Studies, University of Lancaster.

Altermark, N. (2018) *Citizenship Inclusion and Intellectual Disability: Biopolitics Post-Institutionalisation.* Abingdon, Oxon and New York: Routledge (Routledge Advances in Disability Studies).

Arrieta, T. (2022) 'Austerity in the United Kingdom and Its Legacy: Lessons from the COVID-19 Pandemic', *The Economic and Labour Relations Review*, 33(2), pp. 238–255. Available at: https://doi.org/10.1177/10353046221083051.

Atkinson, C. and Robinson, B. (2025) 'Autistic Woman Wrongly Locked Up in Mental Health Hospital for 45 Years', *BBC News*. Available at: https://www.bbc.com/news/articles/cly43png991o (Accessed: 5 March 2025).

Barden, O. (2020a) 'A Cultural History of Learning Difficulties in the Modern Age', in D.T. Mitchell and S.L. Snyder (eds) *A Cultural History of Disability in the Modern Age*. London: Bloomsbury Publishing, pp. 111–132.

Barden, O. and Walden, S.J. (2021) 'The Metanarrative of Learning Disability', in D. Bolt (ed) *Metanarratives of Disability: Culture, Assumed Authority, and the Normative Social Order*. Abingdon, Oxon: Routledge, pp. 77–93.

Bates, K., Goodley, D. and Runswick-Cole, K. (2017) 'Precarious Lives and Resistant Possibilities: The Labour of People with Learning Disabilities in Times of Austerity', *Disability & Society*, 32(2), pp. 160–175. Available at: https://doi.org/10.1080/09687599.2017.1281105.

Bray, K., Braakmann, N. and Wildman, J. (2024) 'Austerity, Welfare Cuts and Hate Crime: Evidence from the UK's Age of Austerity', *Journal of Urban Economics*, 141, p. 103439. Available at: https://doi.org/10.1016/j.jue.2022.103439.

Briant, E., Philo, G. and Watson, N. (2011) *Bad News for Disabled People: How the Newspapers are Reporting Disability*. Glasgow: Strathclyde Centre for Disability Research and Glasgow Media Unit, University of Glasgow. Available at: https://eprints.gla.ac.uk/57499/1/57499.pdf.

Brown, M., James, E. and Hatton, C. (2017) *A Trade in People: The Inpatient Healthcare Economy for People with Learning Disabilities and/or Autism Spectrum Disorder*. Lancaster University, CEDR.

Burch, L. (2022) '"We Shouldn't Be Told to Shut Up, We Should Be Told We Can Speak Out": Reflections on Using Arts-Based Methods to Research Disability Hate Crime', *Qualitative Social Work*, 21(2), pp. 393–412. Available at: https://doi.org/10.1177/14733250211002888.

Care Quality Commission (2020) *Out of Sight – Who Cares? A Review of Restraint, Seclusion and Segregation for Autistic People, and People with a Learning Disability and/or Mental Health Condition*. Newcastle upon Tyne: Care Quality Commission.

Care Quality Commission (2021) *The State of Health Care and Adult Social Care in England 2020/21*. Newcastle upon Tyne: Care Quality Commission.

Care Quality Commission (2022) *Review of Learning Disability Services*. Available at: https://www.cqc.org.uk/publications/themed-inspection/review-learning-disability-services (Accessed: 10 January 2025).

Carpenter, N. (2018) *Austerity's Victims: Adults with a Learning Disability*. CreateSpace Independent Publishing Platform.

Casey, J. (2011) 'Reporter "Haunted" by Abuses', *BBC*. Available at: https://www.bbc.co.uk/panorama/hi/front_page/newsid_9501000/9501531.stm (Accessed: 10 January 2025).

Challenging Behaviour Foundation (2024) *The School Prison Cells*. Challenging Behaviour Foundation. Available at: https://www.challengingbehaviour.org.uk/news/the-school-prison-cells/ (Accessed: 10 January 2025).

Committee of Public Accounts (2025) *DWP Customer Service and Accounts 2023–24*. HC 354. London: House of Commons. Available at: https://committees.parliament.uk/publications/46441/documents/235266/default/ (Accessed: 31 January 2025).

Darwin, C. (1871) *The Descent of Man*. Princeton, NJ: Princeton University Press.

Department of Health (2001) *Valuing People: A New Strategy for Learning Disability for the 21st Century*. Norwich: The Stationery Office.

Department of Health and Social Security / Welsh Office (1971) *Better Services for the Mentally Handicapped*. White Paprt Cmnd 4683. London: HMSO.

Drinkwater, C. (2015) 'Supported Living and the Production of Individuals', in *Foucault and the Government of Disability*. 2nd edn. Ann Arbor: University of Michigan Press, pp. 229–244.

Forrester-Jones, R. *et al.* (2021) 'The Impact of Austerity Measures on People with Intellectual Disabilities in England', *Journal of Long Term Care*, pp. 241–255. Available at: https://doi.org/10.31389/jltc.59.

Foucault, M. (1980) *Power/Knowledge: Selected Interviews and Other Writings 1972–1977*. New York: Pantheon Books.

Gates, B. (2019) 'Subjection of People with Learning Disabilities in the UK: Commentary on Indifference of a Devalued Group', *British Journal of Learning Disabilities*, 47(1), pp. 1–4. Available at: https://doi.org/10.1111/bld.12263.

The Guardian Datablog (2012) 'Disability Hate Crime Is at Its Highest Level Since Records Began', *The Guardian*, 14 August. Available at: http://www.theguardian.com/news/datablog/2012/aug/14/disability-hate-crime-increase-reported-incidents-data (Accessed: 24 January 2025).

Heslop, P. *et al.* (2013) Confidential Inquiry into premature deaths of people with learning disabilities (CIPOLD). Final Report. Bristol: Norah Fry Research Centre, University of Bristol. Available at: https://www.bristol.ac.uk/media-library/sites/cipold/migrated/documents/fullfinalreport.pdf (Accessed: 31 January 2025).

Hindmarch, H. (1992) *Lisieux Hall and the Provision of Services to People with Learning Difficulties in Lancashire*. MA Dissertation. Lancashire Polytechnic. Available at: http://www.lancslearningdisabilityinstitutions.org.uk/content/catalogue_item/heather-hindmarch/calderstones-brockhall-examples-institutional-care (Accessed: 7 November 2017).

Inquest.org.uk (2015) 'Jury Found Neglect Contributed to the Death of 18 Year Old Connor Sparrowhawk', *Inquest*. Available at: https://www.inquest.org.uk/connor-sparrowhawk-inquest-conclusions (Accessed: 10 January 2025).

Learning Disability England (2025) *NHS Priorities: Learning Disability England's Rep Body Respond*. Available at: https://www.learningdisabilityengland.org.uk/news/latest-news/nhs-priorities-response-from-learning-disability-englands-rep-body/ (Accessed: 10 February 2025).

LeDeR (2017) *The Learning Disabilities Mortality Review (LeDeR) programme*. Bristol: University of Bristol Norah Fry Centre for Disability Studies. Available at: https://bjgp.org/lookup/doi/10.3399/bjgp18X697313 (Accessed: 31 January 2025).

Liverpool Echo (2015) 'Brutality of Bedroom Tax Exposed in Disgraceful Images of Disabled Merseysider', *Liverpool Echo*, 22 August. Available at: http://www.liverpoolecho.co.uk/news/liverpool-news/brutality-bedroom-tax-exposed-disgraceful-9911421 (Accessed: 31 January 2025).

Malli, M.A. *et al.* (2018) 'Austerity and the Lives of People with Learning Disabilities: A Thematic Synthesis of Current Literature', *Disability & Society*, 33(9), pp. 1412–1435. Available at: https://doi.org/10.1080/09687599.2018.1497950.

McCausland, R. and Baldry, E. (2017) '"I Feel Like I Failed Him by Ringing the Police": Criminalising Disability in Australia', *Punishment & Society*, 19(3), pp. 290–309. Available at: https://doi.org/10.1177/1462474517696126.

McDermott, R., Goldman, S. and Varenne, H. (2006) 'The Cultural Work of Learning Disabilities', *Educational Researcher*, 35(6), pp. 12–17. Available at: https://doi.org/10.3102/0013189X035006012.

Mencap (2016) *Employment – What We Think*. London: Mencap.

Mencap (2021) *People with a Learning Disability and/or Autism Restrained Over 100,000 Times – Equivalent to Once Every 12 Minutes – in Modern-Day Asylums*. Mencap. Available at: https://www.mencap.org.uk/press-release/people-learning-disability-andor-autism-restrained-over-100000-times-equivalent-once (Accessed: 10 January 2025).

Morris, S. (2017) 'Care Home Directors Convicted Over "Horrific" Learning Disability Regime', *The Guardian*, 7 June. Available at: https://www.theguardian.com/society/2017/jun/07/care-home-directors-convicted-over-devon-learning-disability-regime (Accessed: 10 January 2025).

Mudie, K. (2013) 'Bedroom Tax: Iain Duncan Smith Lives Rent Free in £2Million Country Home with at Least FOUR Spare Bedrooms', *The Mirror*, 30 March. Available at: http://www.mirror.co.uk/news/uk-news/bedroom-tax-iain-duncan-smith-1794517 (Accessed: 31 January 2025).

Nirje, B. (1982) *The Basis and Logic of the Normalisation Principle*. Toronto: Sixth International Congress of IASSMD.

Royal Commission on the Care and Control of the Feeble-Minded (1908) *Report of the Royal Commission on the Care and Control of the Feeble-Minded*. London: HMSO, Royal Commission on the Care and Control of the Feeble-Minded.

Ryan, S. (2017) *Justice for Laughing Boy: Connor Sparrowhawk – A Death by Indifference*. London and Philadelphia: Jessica Kingsley Publishers.

Simpson, M.K. (2018) *Modernity and the Appearance of Idiocy: Intellectual Disability as a Regime of Truth*. New York and Lampeter: Edwin Mellen Press.

Social Finance (2025) *Independent Advocacy for Independent Lives*. London: Social Finance, The Henry Smith Charity. Available at: https://www.socialfinance.org.uk/assets/documents/Independent-advocacy-for-independent-lives.pdf (Accessed: 10 February 2025).

Spivakovsky, C. (2017) 'Governing Freedom Through Risk: Locating the Group Home in the Archipelago of Confinement and Control', *Punishment & Society*, 19(3), pp. 366–383. Available at: https://doi.org/10.1177/1462474517703968.

Stewart, D. (2017) 'Researching the Uncomfortable', in *Social History of Learning Disability Conference*. Milton Keynes: Open University.

Taylor, S. (2011) 'Beasts of Burden', *Qui Parle*, 19(2), pp. 191–222. Available at: https://doi.org/10.5250/quiparle.19.2.0191.

Trent, J.W. (1994) *Inventing the Feeble Mind: A History of Mental Retardation in the United States*. Berkeley: University of California Press.

Unlocking the Past (2010a) *Bath Routines*. Available at: https://web.archive.org/web/20100929091035/http:/www.unlockingthepast.org.uk:80/index/archives/view_archives/89/ (Accessed: 10 January 2025).

Unlocking the Past (2010b) *Refusing Bath*. Available at: https://web.archive.org/web/20100929164634/http:/www.unlockingthepast.org.uk:80/index/archives/view_archives/90/ (Accessed: 10 January 2025).

Walmsley, J. and Jarrett, S. (eds) (2021) *Intellectual Disability in the Twentieth Century: Transnational Perspectives on People, Policy and Practice*. Bristol: Policy Press.

Wolfensberger, W. (1972) *Normalization: The Principle of Normalization in Human Services*. Toronto: National Institute of Mental Retardation, Leonard Crainford.

Wright, D. and Digby, A. (eds) (1996) *From Idiocy to Mental Deficiency: Historical Perspectives on People with Learning Difficulties*. London: Routledge.

5 Human *and* Posthuman

Introduction

As we saw in the earlier chapters of this book, notions of the independent, rational thinker lie at the heart of conceptualisations of both the human and of learning disability. Academic and legal definitions, for example, typically frame learning disability in terms of what learning-disabled people are deemed not capable of, in comparison to a notional normal rational, intelligent person. This chapter seeks to trouble such definitions and distinctions. People labelled with learning disabilities give us good reasons to question our notions of normalcy and our relationships to it, including our idolisation of the Vitruvian rational thinker (Cockain, 2024). In that spirit, this final chapter first critiques the contemporary fixation with rationality and then takes the book beyond the present and its current norms, adopting a Posthumanist perspective to consider the future of humanity and of learning disability. It argues that now more than ever, in these times of crisis, we need to think about people in terms of relationships, not individuals; to accept rather than pathologise our inability to match the neoliberal imperative; to embrace and thrive upon that which many of us currently fear, regarding the disabled bodymind as the rule, not the exception (Mitchell and Snyder, 2015).

The chapter reviews current research which suggests that not only can learning-disabled people participate meaningfully in research and knowledge production, but also that knowledge and perspectives elicited through such research can help us appreciate our interdependence and address pressing global concerns such as the Earth's accelerating climate catastrophe. This might be considered an attempt to short-circuit the perpetual cycle of optimism/pessimism in conceptualising learning disability (Jarrett and Tilley, 2022), through thinking in terms of our common humanity rather than our perceived differences. Conceptualisations of learning disability are historically contingent, and the idea of intelligence as something that defines membership of the human race is itself relatively recent. If learning disability has an historical point

DOI: 10.4324/9781003411925-5

of origin, one implication is that prior to that moment it went unrecognised. A second implication is that the notion of learning disability might vanish in the future. As C.F. Goodey says, "If the past is a foreign country where they do things differently, there is a future country where they do things differently and better" (Goodey, 2011: 4). This chapter imagines a path to this future country. It begins by critiquing the privileged place of rational thinking in conceptions of what it means to be human, before offering an alternative, posthuman perspective. This perspective is used to explore the ways in which recognition of our interdependencies with each other, with nature and with technology, might productively inform our futures.

Rationality, Dysrationalia and the Nature of Reasoning

Histories of learning disability and histories of intelligence – indeed, we could say histories of humanity – show unequivocally that learning disabilities are sociocultural constructs. This is inarguable. Back in 1993, the eminent psychologist Keith Stanovich showed how easy it was to invent a new learning disability. And when we invent a new learning disability, we invent more than just a new diagnostic category; we effectively create a new "kind" of person – the kind of person who fits within the category we have just created, usually because we want to surveil and hence control them (Hacking, 2004). As we have seen, Henry H. Goddard did exactly this when he invented the moron. Stanovich took a different approach. He wanted to critique psycho-medical professionals' propensity to create new diagnoses, and the conceptual foundations such diagnostic categories rested upon. He pointed out that all anyone needs to do to invent a new learning disability – and so a new kind of person – is to pick an aspect of thinking or intelligence that can purportedly be measured, measure it, and find a statistically significant discrepancy between that score and the person's score on a standardised IQ test. To illustrate his case, he invented a new, spoof learning disability called *dysrationalia*. Aping the format used for existing specific learning difficulties like dyslexia, he defined dysrationalia as an enduring disposition characterised by

> [t]he inability to think and behave rationally despite adequate intelligence. It is a general term that refers to a heterogeneous group of disorders manifested by significant difficulties in belief formation, in the assessment of belief consistency, and/or in the determination of action to achieve one's goals. Although dysrationalia may occur concomitantly with other handicapping conditions (e.g. sensory impairment), it is not the result of those conditions. The key diagnostic criterion for dysrationalia is a level of rationality, as demonstrated

> in thinking and behaviour, that is significantly below the level of the individual's intellectual capacity (as determined by an individually administered IQ test).
>
> (Stanovich, 1993: 503)

Stanovich gave some helpful examples to illustrate apparent real-life cases of dysrationalia. These included a survey on the paranormal beliefs of members of a Mensa club in Canada. Mensa members must evidence high IQs, yet in this Canadian branch 56% reported believing in the existence of extraterrestrial visitors and 44% reported believing in astrology: beliefs for which "there is no valid evidence" (Stanovich, 1993). In other words, a large number of Mensa members could be diagnosed as *dysrationalistic* in a way directly analogous to the way a person with an average or better IQ score yet low literacy scores on standardised tests would be diagnosed as dyslexic. Stanovich's point was that average or even high IQ does not inoculate people against "significant difficulties in belief formation", because the supposedly intelligent people in these examples readily formed and maintained irrational beliefs: beliefs which lack any convincing evidence on which to base them. So, the critique here is twofold. Firstly, Stanovich demonstrates that it is very easy to create new kinds of learning disability, and that the kinds of new learning disability created will inevitably reflect the interests and prejudices of the people creating them. People or cultures who value rational thought are far more likely to invent a learning disability characterised by an apparent inability to think rationally than people or cultures who don't. The irony here relates to the second part of the critique: that even the most supposedly intelligent people – as measured by IQ tests – who we would presume to be the most rational thinkers – often think irrationally. In some ways, Stanvoich's work therefore acts as a precursor to the kinds of critique of conventional conceptualisations of rational thought offered by Mercier and Sperber in *The Enigma of* Reason, which we encountered in Chapter 2. It would seem that rational thought truly is an ableist ideal nobody can live up to (Goodley, 2014).

A great deal of research in cognitive psychology has tried to explain why this is so. Some of the most influential work has come from the subfield of *heuristics and biases*. This field examines the role of knowledge bases on rationality. That is, the field is concerned with the way the autonomous mind retrieves overlearned knowledge derived from experience and how this knowledge impinges on rationality. The most well-known work in this field is probably that of Nobel Prize winner Daniel Kahneman, summarised in the popular bestseller *Thinking Fast and Slow* (Khaneman, 2011). Kahneman's view – in a nutshell – is that what he perceives as flaws in the design of the machinery of cognition predispose people to irrational thought. He argues that fast T1 thinking – which is impressionistic, rapid and hence error-prone – is our default setting. Yet rational thinking demands fast T1 and slow T2: the analytic mind must consciously reason, overruling the intuitive, impulsive one. Unfortunately, the argument goes, people tend not to engage T2 – dubbed "the lazy controller" – because it is slow and effortful. This inherent bias towards fast, low-effort thinking and our aversion to considered analysis is responsible for significant flaws: for example, that people tend to overgeneralise from past experience, and tend not to modify their beliefs in the face of new evidence or information, so that their attitudes and actions frequently lack a rational basis. Stanovich *et al.* (2011) observe that researchers in heuristics and biases have repeatedly demonstrated that people, regardless of intelligence, habitually violate the precepts of rationality: they tend towards confirmation bias, they do not test hypotheses thoroughly, they do not accurately calibrate their beliefs to the evidence available, and they over-project their own opinions onto others. They go on to argue that individual differences in rationality may be partially attributable to variations in intelligence, but that high intelligence alone does not inoculate against irrationality – as in the case of the Canadian Mensa members. They claim that many different studies involving thousands of subjects have indicated that measures of intelligence display only moderate to weak or near-zero correlations with thinking dispositions associated with rational thought.

In some previous work, I tried to use this logic to explain why non-disabled people so often harbour irrational beliefs and prejudices about disabled people (Barden, 2014). I made the case that the influence of negative emotions, stereotypes and representations associated with disability and disabled people, like fear, pity and disgust, would tend to dominate and disrupt people's reactions to impairment. These metanarratives of disability would thus help form the foundations for stigma (Bolt, 2012) and the thinking disposition known as prejudice: "irrational, pervasive and enduring sentiment" (Katz, 1991: 127) which results in hostility towards, and avoidance of, minority groups – including, perhaps even especially, people with learning disabilities. Since then, other cognitive psychologists have argued that it is Kahneman's model that is flawed, rather than the machinery of cognition. Kahneman's model presumes a Humanist, individual thinker, reasoning in their own head in order to come up with sound reasons and strong arguments. Following from this, the diagnosis of dysrationalia I made in regard to attitudes towards disability suggested a cure based on the dual-thinking T1–T2 model; to encourage people to take the time to think carefully and logically about disability, and how their opinions have been shaped by the relevant metanarratives (Barden and Walden, 2021), in order to arrive at new beliefs and attitudes. Unfortunately, the evidence from cognitive psychology indicates that almost everybody performs poorly at this kind of reasoning. Even worse, when they do reason in this manner, they tend to come up with reasons which entrench their existing beliefs. And worse again, they seem to be very bad at judging the quality of the reasons they come up with.

These problems, together with advances in our understanding of the nature of rational thought, tell us that the cure for disability dysrationalia needs to be modified. We need to move away from the notion of the Vitruvian rational thinker, bound and isolated in his box, towards a notion of people thinking together, and so learning from and with each other. In *The Enigma of Reason*, Mercier and Sperber, drawing on evidence from Aristotle to Jürgen Habermas[1] to a wealth of contemporary experiments, make a compelling case for reasoning being a social rather than individualist endeavour. The same body of evidence that highlights those major flaws in individualistic reasoning shows us that most people are very good at evaluating other people's arguments. They will only accept other people's arguments if those arguments are strong. And, happily, they will tend to accept from other people reasons which challenge their beliefs, provided again that those reasons are strong enough.

What this means is that people depend on other people in order to be able to reason well and change their minds. We are interdependent thinkers, not independent thinkers. Reasoning is social; it happens best when we do it together. Mercier and Sperber's interactionist model of reasoning therefore offers a much more effective potential cure for dysrationalia. Rather than relying on individuals to reflect in isolation on their prejudicial attitudes – which was always perhaps rather wishful thinking – this cure involves dialogue. If we can offer, in dialogue, strong enough reasons for non-disabled people to consider learning-disabled people as fully human, then they ought to change their minds: "evidence shows how, even in the moral and political realms, argumentation . . . may allow participants to form more accurate moral judgements and citizens to form more enlightened opinions" (Mercier and Sperber, 2018: 11).

This is another way of saying we need to co-respond with learning disability, which is of course the object of this book. Somewhat paradoxically, as part of this process, we might need to collectively reason our way into loosening reasoning's grip on conceptualisations of what it means to be human.[2] To use Tim Ingold's phrase, People of Culture – the controlling, psycho-medical professions – have reasoned *about* learning-disabled people and used this reasoning to position learning disability in very particular ways which fit with their preconceptions and predispositions. This is how we have ended up with the plethora of diagnostic categories and thus "kinds" of people Keith Stanovich, Ian Hacking and many others have brought our attention to. People with learning disabilities have been objects rather than subjects in this discourse. They have not been reasoned, or – co-responded with – in dialogue. And so we need to find ways to learn with people with learning disabilities in order to form more accurate moral judgements and more enlightened opinions with them. This may well entail questioning our communicative norms and assumption of rationalistic ideals. After all, as the moral philosopher Christine Korsgaard has said: "Frankly, it's not like you can subtract rationality from a human being and what's left is a dog" (Edmonds and Warburton, 2023). We need to embrace alternative conceptualisations of the human, and one promising option is Posthumanism.

Posthuman Interdependence

In Chapter 2, as well as at the start of this chapter, I made the case for our current understandings of personhood and of learning disability being dominated by a Humanist perspective. In the Humanist perspective, to be considered fully human, one must embody certain characteristics. One must be capable, rational, independent and so on. Those people – and things – who do not embody these characteristics are othered, and usually treated as inferior. Donna Haraway writes of how this has tended to create divisions between nature and society, non-human and human, with these Others having "a remarkable capacity to induce panic in the centers of power and self-certainty" (Haraway, 2013: 10). Here, perhaps we can see not only a contribution to the ontological foundations of Darwin's theory of natural selection, which sets Man apart at the top of the evolutionary tree – in the same way the Bible awarded Man dominion over the Earth and its creatures (Gen 1:26–28), and that during the Renaissance, including da Vinci's lifetime, the rational soul was thought closest to God and purity (Lathrop, 2020) – but also the origins of our tendency to fear and denigrate "gods, machines, animals, monsters, creepy crawlies, women, servants and slaves, and noncitizens in general" (Haraway, 2013). People with learning disabilities have of course been characterised as gods, animals, monsters, servants and slaves, and incapable non-citizens across cultures and time, cementing their position as the ultimate outgroup and leading to inclusion phobia, which is to say a deep-seated perennial aversion to including people with learning disabilities in society (Goodey, 2016). As we've just seen, this phobia might itself be seen to arise from *dysrationalia*, resulting in a failure to think rationally about learning disability.

In recent decades, an alternative perspective to Humanism has emerged, called Posthumanism. This after-humanism conceives of humans in a radically different and much more inclusive and expansive ways. It represents a paradigm shift in thinking about the nature of our species, our identities and our relationships. Posthumanism offers alternative, affirmative models for what it means to be human, and is also a way of thinking about the future. It is less anthropocentric and de-centres the Vitruvian Humanist ideal. Using this perspective, we see capacity, resources and potential as residing in relationships, not individuals. We exist in fellowship: we are all human, and thus share both a common nature and a common predicament. At its heart, Posthumanism is optimistic, contending that although we live in times of crisis, we can meet the challenges of climate change, war, shrinking habitats and so on by reconfiguring our relationships with other, nature and technology. Those people who were othered and seen as disposable under Humanism are centred: women, racial minorities and disabled people, for example, and their knowledges and perspectives are sought and surfaced. People's multiple, intersecting identities are recognised – that it is possible, for instance, to be learning-disabled and gay and religious, all at once – as is our interconnectedness and interdependence with other people as well as other species and nature and ecology. One of Posthumanism's most influential proponents, Rosa Braidotti, conceives a nature–culture continuum (Braidotti, 2013), where our surviving and thriving depends as much upon the bees who pollinate our food crops as the satellites and drones who monitor and perhaps even bring in the harvest. In a similar vein, philosopher of disability Licia Carlson notes:

> Many have celebrated the posthuman condition as one in which the boundaries between human, animal, and machine are contested and blurred. This posthuman age holds the promise of the emergence of new subjectivities and alliances, and of leaving restrictive, exclusionary, and oppressive ideals and practices of older forms of "humanism" behind.
>
> (Carlson, 2023: np)

This is a moment in the book where some caution must temper a rare outbreak of optimism. In the first chapter, I spent some considerable time laying out my position as a highly privileged, white, European, male, middle-aged, middle class, non-disabled academic. I also happen to enjoy keeping fit and participating in endurance events like ultra-running and triathlon. I could be seen to embody many of the characteristics the Vitruvian humanist ideal promotes. And this is precisely why care is needed. Posthumanism has only arrived recently on the theoretical scene. Whilst it does seem to offer opportunities to reorientate our relationships with learning disability and the wider world around us, it also risks entrenching existing exclusions. Although Rosa Braidotti and other scholars of disability and posthumanism have argued that critical Disability Studies align well with posthumanism, because disability has always contravened the traditional classical humanist conception of what it means to be human, there is a danger that posthumanism reinscribes old forms of ableism and dehumanisation, especially if disabled people are excluded from the discussion. Licia Carlson has a particular interest in learning disability, and rightly asks: How can we expect people to adopt a sophisticated, nuanced new perspective called posthumanism if they are still struggling even to be recognised as fully human? She also cautions of the dangers defining the posthuman subject as a particular kind of thinker, able to ponder complex and dynamic processes, as Rosa Braidotti and others have done. Any normative imperative to think in one particular way risks excluding large numbers of people, including people labelled with learning disabilities and other neurodiverse embodiments. Carlson's proposed solution is partly to recognise the common humanity of all people whilst also thinking imaginatively, provocatively and critically about the future; and partly to listen to the stories of those people who have hitherto been dehumanised in imagining posthuman future. Many of these stories illustrate the ways in which rational decisions, embedded in a habitus of ableism, lead to exclusions and oppression, either by design or ignorance (Dokumaci, 2023). Yet they also point towards our interdependent futures.

The recent Coronavirus pandemic is a case in point. It very quickly showed us how interdependent we are and how fragile many of our systems are. Although disabled people bore the brunt, and learning-disabled people in particular fared especially badly, it affected everybody. All of a sudden, we were all fulfilling care responsibilities as well as working; all of a sudden, we were all made aware of how interconnected and vulnerable many of our relationships and systems were; food, transport, medicine – and thanks to Brexit, at the time of writing, the NHS is still experiencing major medication shortages, further underscoring this fragility and interdependence. The switch to remote working, flexible working, video-conferencing, tele-health consultations, the emphasis on well-being and looking after ourselves and each other became the new normal, for many of us. All of these were things that disabled people had been asking for many years, but had been told were not possible, because they were too expensive, too difficult. But it was striking how they immediately became possible – in fact, essential – as soon as non-disabled people needed them. Here was the ableist habitus in action. What doesn't get talked about enough is how innovations like videoconferencing and automated subtitling tend to come from the margins rather than the mainstream. Many technological advances – from text messaging to Siri on mobile phones, for instance – started life as adaptations for disabled people. In other words, they might not exist, or would probably not have been invented or become mainstream as quickly as they have, were it not for disability. Non-disabled people have disabled people to thank for many of the devices and practices they rely on so heavily to conduct their everyday lives. This is an example of our interdependence on each other as well as on technology.

Such advances and adaptations, and our responses to the Coronavirus pandemic, highlight opportunities for the flourishing of expression, creativity, resourcefulness, sturdiness and interdependence that Rosemarie Garland-Thomson, amongst others, has written about in arguing the case for the conservation of disability (Garland-Thomson, 2015; Barden *et al.*, 2023). The essential idea here is that rather than simply being a problem to be fixed, disability is an inevitable part of being human – remember the truism that we all become disabled if we live long enough. But more than that, disability is generative resource – one that benefits society and communities. These benefits come from adapting the world and the ways we live in it. Early on in the pandemic, disability scholar and activist Alice Wong characterised disabled people as "cyborgs and oracles" in her Disability Visibility Project blog. When confronted with the idea of a cyborg, perhaps for many of us the first thing that springs to mind is a futuristic representation from science fiction. But there is a strong case for saying that many cyborgs already live among us – and that they are in fact disabled people. Wong referred to disabled people like herself as *cyborgs* because of their frequent intimate relationships with technology; she uses a machine called a bi-pap to breathe, which must continually draw power from the battery of her wheelchair. She also called disabled people *oracles* because they know what it means to be vulnerable and interdependent, and therefore have a vision of what a future in which are increasingly both precarious and interdependent might be like. These adaptive ways of living arise from disability, and point towards ways of living harmoniously in the future. Alice spoke of finding "strength and hope from communities organizing mutual aid and providing care for one another" (Wong, 2020). Alice argued that this is why everybody should listen to disabled people; and of course, COVID-19 was never and is not the only threat humanity faces. War, climate change and biodiversity loss continue to render us all vulnerable and life on Earth increasingly precarious. Arseli Dokumaci writes of how "Impaired, sick, painful bodies, mad selves, debilitated populations, vulnerable beings and threatened organisms live in environments that for them are shrunken and shrinking" (Dokumaci, 2023: 7), and how this necessitates new ways of living. And so it is more important than ever to listen to – learn with – disabled people – because they can show humanity how to live in the future because they are already adapting to it by how they live in the present.

This is one place where we might need to collectively reason ourselves into loosening rational thought's grip on conceptualisations of what it means to be human as we recalibrate our relationships with each other and the natural world. Attempts to dominate each other and nature have created problems so huge they are existential threats not just to us but also to much of the natural world. This tells us that it is imperative for us to move away from hierarchical, rational thinking which pits animals in competition with each other, humans in competition with each other, and humans and animals in competition with each other to rule the world. Whereas up until now, disabled people have been doubly othered, dehumanised and also perceived as incompatible with the natural environment (Ojrzyńska, 2023), we need to recognise both our fellowship as human beings and the necessity of living in harmony with each other and with nature. Humanist arguments tend to appeal to cognitive ability and assumed rationalism which aims to elevate some non-human animals like apes, collie dogs and grey parrots to the same moral status as some humans, such as those with labels of severe or profound learning disabilities. This raises the question of why it is necessary to set people in competition with each other and with animals, in terms of deserving full moral treatment, with each other in the first place. The philosopher Peter Singer, for example, has famously argued that some non-human animals ought to be regarded as having the same moral status as some humans, whilst others have positioned some humans as less deserving of full moral status than some non-human animals. This kind of thinking will inevitably result in some form of hierarchy. Normal people are placed above – in Singer's terms – subnormal humans, who are put on a level with parrots, pigs and dolphins (Jaworska, 2010; Kittay and Carlson, 2010). But as climate change and habitat devastation continue apace, we cannot disentangle the disablement of humans – which is increasingly likely for all of us in these precarious times – from the disablement of other species and their lifeworlds, which we are, the scientists tell us unequivocally, largely responsible for causing. Rather than saving the planet, we need to save each other, working together and with each other. Accessible and secure futures are possible, if we make them happen, and we are all vulnerable if we don't.

What ecology and the climate crises are showing us as that we are interdependent with non-human animals, just as they are interdependent with each other. Anemones on the Great Barrier Reef are mutually dependent on the clown fish that live there; the reef itself is dependent on healthy mangrove swamps on the shoreline; the health of the mangroves depends on what happens upstream in the farmlands, the plains and right on up to the mountains and the atmosphere. These apparently distinct entities and systems are in fact profoundly interdependent. And, to take a different example, humans won't survive without bees. This has nothing whatsoever to do with their cognitive ability. We simply can't feed ourselves without them. We need to take action to ensure that our activities do not make bees extinct. If they die out, we will too, within a decade. In that sense, they are now dependent on us not exterminating them (although originally of course they were better off without us interfering). Now, I am not trying to make an instrumental, means–end argument here. I am not saying that bees, other animals and plants only exist for our benefit. What I am suggesting is that pitting humans and non-human animals against each other, or trying to locate them in some kind of intelligence-based hierarchy, is misguided because species are interdependent, irrespective of cognitive ability. And so cognitive ability is not appropriate as a measure of the value of life.

As such, we need theories of disability and of personhood that eradicate human exceptionalism and account for our complex, multispecies environment (Linett, 2023). This theory also needs to account for the fact that human lives are interdependent. People labelled with learning disabilities are not simply dependent on other humans; other humans depend on them too, for what they can teach about humanity; about callousness and disregard, as well as care, agency, compassion and community. Posthumanism seems to offer some promise here. One way it does this is to highlight the limitations of rational, Humanist thought, pointing to the need to collectively reason ourselves into loosening rational thought's grip on conceptualisations of what it means to be human. We need to recognise that rather than emotions corrupting rational thought, as Kahneman and others would have it, thinking is inextricably bound up with emotions. And those of us who are learning-disabled, or consider themselves allies or advocates for people with learning disabilities, need to harness those emotions in order to persuade others to accept the full human status of people with learning disabilities, giving strong reasons in dialogue with non-disabled people. One potential way to do this is through the power of emotional communities.

Learning Disability and Emotional Communities

Usually when we talk about disability history, we talk about facts and events: what happened to who, and when, and often about how terrible it was, as I have done in previous chapters of this book. Sometimes when we talk about disability history, we talk about conceptualisations of disability and disabled people, and how we think they differ from current conceptualisations, perhaps giving examples of disabled people being more accepted in pre-industrial communities, or even worshipped as gods – something we don't see much of today. I am going to talk about something different in this final section, something we don't tend to talk about when we talk about disability history. I am going to tell a story of how doing learning disability history research can bring people – disabled and not – together as an emotional community, and the power that such a community can have. I present this emotional community, of which I am a member, as one example of the kind of posthumanist interdependence I have been arguing for so far in this chapter. It is a community where we "labour together to construct affirmative ethical and political practices" (Braidotti, 2019). The thing that brought this emotional community together was a shared interest in researching learning disability history. Our emotional community comprises people with learning disabilities and people without. It also includes non-human animals and even inanimate objects, which might initially seem far-fetched, but which I will try to justify. In addition to describing this emotional community, I will try to show how such a community might be harnessed to generate positive change. But first, I will explain how this community came about. As we near the conclusion of this book, it seems apt to reach back into the past and – in the words of one of my learning-disabled co-researchers – bring it into the future (Barden *et al.*, 2022).

At the 2019 Disability and Disciplines conference hosted by the Centre for Cultural and Disability Studies at Liverpool Hope University, I co-presented a paper on researching the history of learning disability. My co-presenters were my co-researchers from The Brain Charity in Liverpool, some of whom have learning disabilities and some of whom are family members and advocates without learning disabilities. I co-presented a similar paper with another group of co-researchers from the University of South Wales at the annual Social History of Learning Disability conference at the Open University a couple of weeks later. Our project had been a micro-history of one lady with learning disability. She was called Antonia Grandoni, who you may remember from Chapter 2. To quickly recap, Antonia spent much of her life, between about 1840 and 1870, incarcerated in a hospital in Milan after being diagnosed with microcephalic idiocy. We studied her because Dr William Ireland, a prominent expert on idiocy at the time, included her as a case study in a book we discovered in a digital archive (Ireland, 1877). We thought that analysing and interpreting Antonia's story could tell us a lot not just about living with a learning disability in the mid-19th century, but also about living with a learning disability today (Magnússon, 2021). Unbeknownst to us, in the audience at Disability and Disciplines were academics from the University of Iceland, who were in the early stages of their own participatory project on the history of learning disability, a micro-history of a lady called Bjargey Kristjánsdóttir, known as Bíbí (Stefánsdóttir *et al.*, 2025). Even though their lives were separated by many decades and the breadth of a continent, Antonia and Bíbí's existences seemed to bear a number of strong resemblances, being characterised by segregation, neglect and longings for emotional connection. These two teams of researchers met with a third, similar team based at the Open University at the Social History of Learning Disability conference in July 2023. That day was itself very emotional. We talked a lot about the emotions we felt when doing research about the history of learning disability. These run the whole gamut from shock, disgust and outrage at the ways people with learning disabilities have been – and continue to be – treated – to defiance and pride, to taking delight in sharing stories and producing creative works to show what we've found and what we feel about it, to devotion to the cause of advocacy. A distinctive paradox of doing this kind of participatory research is how harrowing moments are juxtaposed with moments of laughter and joy. The emotionally charged atmosphere of the day helped to make manifest a sense of community which had hitherto been latent. One of the Icelandic scholars, Sola Ólafsdóttir, gave a presentation on how the concept of emotional community had been used in that team's analysis of Bíbí's life, and together these things led us to begin to theorise ourselves as an emotional community.

The concept of emotional community comes from Barbara Rosenwein, a professor of medieval history at Loyola University, Chicago. In 2002, Rosenwein wrote a landmark article in the *American Historical Review* "Worrying about Emotions in History". In it, she introduces and defines emotional communities, and thereby affords us a useful way of thinking about how communities function. Roswenwein's definition of emotional communities explains that although all humans possess an inherent, biological capacity to experience emotions, how we label, express and react to emotions is not simply a personal matter, but is shaped by culture and context. For example, there is evidence to suggest the people from Germany and Israel are often highly sensitive to expressions of anger, whereas people from Greece are more likely to be highly sensitive to expressions of sadness (Van Kleef *et al.*, 2016). The cultures and contexts which influence our experiences and expressions of emotions help us form emotional communities. Emotional communities are what give emotions names, values and respect; they are where we make sense of the emotions we feel, by sharing them with people who experience and evaluate them in similar ways. They are somewhat similar to speech communities, where people use language in specific ways in specific contexts (Matsumoto, 2013; Stefánsdóttir and Ólafsdóttir, 2021). Emotional communities therefore embody systems – or perhaps cultures – of feeling. Our emotional community is one in which we feel, value and respond to emotions relating to learning disability in similar ways. We tend to feel outrage and joy about the same sorts of things, even though as human beings are responses to the world around us are individual and shaped by many more influences than just this one community.

Rather than simply asserting that we are an emotional community and leaving it at that, we have already begun to mobilise the power this community affords us. One of the most significant things we have done is collectively write a scholarly journal article about our community and what it does (Barden *et al.*, 2025). And one of the most powerful things it does it provide a safe space for people to share their experiences of learning disability. Helena, another Icelandic colleague, provided us with an excellent example of this. She told us of how one of her learning-disabled co-researchers felt that by sitting with people who were remembering complicated things and sharing their feelings about them, she was able to talk about her feelings for the first time in her life. Before that, she had been afraid of talking about her feelings, because they are difficult. Take a moment to imagine that: not only being in your 20s and talking about your feelings for the first time in your life, but what that might unlock when you did. And expressing emotions is surely at least as much of a human quality – if not more so – than a capacity for rational thought, although not one restricted to humans (Shek-Noble and Jones, 2023).

We are emotional beings, and it is often the emotions we encounter in doing learning disability research that make it what it is, and not any attempt at objective, rational, disinterested, scientific thought. It is also worth pausing here to note how our emotional community operates in such a way as to enable us to do things like collectively write a journal article. It is worth it because our ways of working reflect the posthuman perspective advocated for above. Firstly, in recognition of our fellowship, everybody's contributions, and thereby every person, is afforded equal worth, no matter how that contribution is made. Some of us speak very little, if at all, for example, yet still contributed and were credited with equal authorship of the journal article. In other words, in listening to the stories of those people who have hitherto been dehumanised, we recognised our common humanity. Secondly, some but not all of our meetings were highly technologically dependent, using videoconferencing and AI transcription. Other meetings were held face-to-face, and reported back on to the rest of the community. This meant people could participate in ways that suited them. This aspect of our work highlights our interdependence with technology; although some of us use a variety of devices, platforms and practices in prolific and even sometimes quite sophisticated ways, even those of us who don't even use email rely on digital technology to have their stories heard. Thirdly, these ways of working allowed quite profound stories of our interdependence with nature to emerge. The Icelandic team told of how during their investigations, they were gifted Bíbí's 145,000-word handwritten autobiography, and subsequently discovered Bíbí's diary and numerous poems that she had written. These texts, alongside other artefacts such as Bíbí's extensive doll collection, revealed a complex and insightful interior emotional life. Like Antonia Grandoni, her Italian counterpart, Bíbí often seemed to crave emotional connections and caring human relationships. As it was, many of her most intimate emotional connections appeared to be with the animals and nature that surrounded her in rural Iceland. It might be tempting to attribute this solely to her ostracisation and isolation, but this finding reflects other research in which people with learning disabilities, living in the city and with active social lives and fulfilling human relationships, report feelings of profound relationships with nature which reflect multispecies entanglement (Clive, 2021). So, here is a third key element of the posthuman perspective: recognition of our interdependence on nature, not just for survival but also for emotional sustenance. The fourth and final element of this posthumanist picture brings us full circle to learning *with* learning disability. It is an example of changing people's minds through dialogue. Sola, one of the Icelandic researchers on the Bíbí project, tells a story of a colleague of theirs who travels the world, and wherever he goes, he connects with the history department of a university. He gives lectures where he tells people about Bíbí and her life. One time, at the end of a lecture on Bíbí he is giving in Japan, making the case for her as a person with full moral standing, he notices that one of the Japanese professors has gone very quiet. He wonders why, and it turns out in the end that the Japanese professor, who had had no interest in learning disability before, is crying. So, on the one hand, this might be a way of extending the membership of our community; getting new people to experience similar emotions as we do in response to learning disability. To care about learning disability and learning-disabled people. On the other hand, it is also a way to make things happen. If you can get people to care about something so much that they cry, maybe you have already made an important change that influences them to think and act differently in the future.

Conclusion

In this chapter, we have turned from past and the present, and looked towards the future. The chapter has made a case for thinking differently about both learning disability and what it means to be human. I have argued, firstly, that traditional, Humanist conceptions of the human have not only led to the dehumanisation of people with learning disabilities, but also permitted an ever-expanding array of diagnoses and therefore kinds of person to proliferate, whom other kinds of person have sought to control. Following on from this, I have argued that the drive for dominion over both certain kinds of people and the Earth and its finite resources has contributed significantly to the existential crisis we and our fellow creatures currently face. So far, so bad. However, what we have now is an opportunity to re-evaluate and reorientate our relationships with learning disability, what it means to be human, and the world around us.

Posthumanism affords us one perspective from which to do this. In this perspective, rather than conceptualising the ideal or even normal person as an individualistic, isolated, rational thinker, we recognise our intricate interdependencies. Asylum medical superintendents, psychologists, psychiatrists, neuroscientists and a whole host of allied professions have or do all depend on people with learning disabilities for their careers (Swain and French, 2008). Non-disabled academics like me need people with learning disabilities to research with and write with and about. These examples might be trite, but they are true. But more profoundly than that, as I have tried to demonstrate throughout this book, we all depend on each other for our sense of self and even our continued existence. People with learning disabilities can teach other humans a lot about themselves and how to coexist with each other and with nature. With this in mind, I have reiterated the case for people with learning disabilities to be regarded as having full and equal moral status with other human beings (Carlson, 2023). More than that, I have tried to show how disabled people, including learning disabled people, can show us how to live together harmoniously, in fellowship, in the future. Not just as technologically dependent cyborgs and oracles, but as members of communities who provide care and support for each other. Finally, I have shown how learning disability activism, rooted in such a community, has the power and potential to make the world a better place.

Notes

1 It is worth noting here that Habermas' philosophy was shaped by childhood responses his own disability – a cleft palate resulting in a speech impairment – as well as his doubts over instrumental rationality.

2 It may seem paradoxical, but even 400 years ago, Blaise Pascal argued that the end point of rationality is to demonstrate the limits of rationality.

References

Barden, O. (2014) 'Dysrationalia: An Institutional Learning Disability?', in D. Bolt (ed) *Changing Social Attitudes Toward Disability: Perspectives from Historical, Cultural, and Educational Studies*. Abingdon, Oxon: Routledge, pp. 142–152.

Barden, O. and Walden, S.J. (2021) 'The Metanarrative of Learning Disability', in D. Bolt (ed) *Metanarratives of Disability: Culture, Assumed Authority, and the Normative Social Order*. Abingdon, Oxon: Routledge, pp. 77–93.

Barden, O. *et al.* (2022) 'Antonia's Story: Bringing the Past into the Future', *British Journal of Learning Disabilities*, 50(2), pp. 258–269. Available at: https://doi.org/10.1111/bld.12447.

Barden, O. *et al.* (2023) 'Disability and Social Inclusion: Lessons from the Pandemic', *Social Inclusion*, 11(1), pp. 1–4. Available at: https://doi.org/10.17645/si.v11i1.6612.

Barden, O. *et al.* (2025) 'Emotionally Entwined Narratives: A Polyphonic Trialogue on Learning Disability History Research', *Frontiers in Sociology*, 10.

Bolt, D. (2012) 'Social Encounters, Cultural Representation and Critical Avoidance', in *Routledge Handbook of Disability Studies*. Routledge.

Braidotti, R. (2013) *The Posthuman*. Cambridge and Malden, MA: Polity Press.

Braidotti, R. (2019) *Posthuman Knowledge*. Cambridge: Polity Press.

Carlson, L. (2023) 'Intellectual Disability, Dehumanization, and the Fate of "the Human"', *The Journal of Philosophy of Disability*, 3, pp. 47–70. Available at: https://doi.org/10.5840/jpd2023101121.

Clive, R. (2021) 'Panarchy 3: River of the Sea: Towards a Learning-Disabled-Led Ecological Performance Practice', *Journal of Literary & Cultural Disability Studies*, 15(3), pp. 329–346. Available at: https://doi.org/10.3828/jlcds.2021.26.

Cockain, A. (2024) *Learning Disability and Everyday Life*. Abingdon, Oxon: Routledge.

Dokumaci, A. (2023) *Activist Affordances: How Disabled People Improvise More Habitable Worlds*. Durham and London: Duke University Press.

Edmonds, D. and Warburton, N. (n.d.) 'Christine Korsgaard on the Status of Animals', *Philosophy Bites*. Available at: https://nigelwarburton.typepad.com/philosophy_bites//2015/02/christine-korsgaard-on-the-status-of-animals.html (Accessed: 2 November 2023).

Garland-Thomson, R. (2015) 'Human Biodiversity Conservation: A Consensual Ethical Principle', *The American Journal of Bioethics*, 15(6), pp. 13–15. Available at: https://doi.org/10.1080/15265161.2015.1028663.

Goodey, C.F. (2011) *A History of Intelligence and 'Intellectual Disability': The Shaping of Psychology in Early Modern Europe*. 1st edn. London: Routledge. Available at: https://doi.org/10.4324/9781315564838.

Goodey, C.F. (2016) *Learning Disability and Inclusion Phobia: Past, Present, Future*. 1st edn. London and New York: Taylor and Francis (Routledge Advances in the Medical Humanities). Available at: https://doi.org/10.4324/9780203556658.

Goodley, D. (2014) *Dis/ability Studies: Theorising Disablism and Ableism*. London: Routledge. Available at: https://hope.primo.exlibrisgroup.com/discovery/fulldisplay?docid=cdi_askewsholts_vlebooks_9781134060900&context=PC&vid=44HOP_INST:VU1&lang=en&search_scope=MyInst_and_CI&adaptor=Primo%20Central&tab=Everything&query=any,contains,Goodley,%20D.%20(2014)%20Dis%2Fability%20Studies:%20Theorising%20disablism%20and%20ableism.%20London:%20Routledge.&offset=0 (Accessed: 1 November 2023).

Hacking, I. (2004) *Historical Ontology*. Cambridge, MA: Harvard University Press.

Haraway, D.J. (2013) *When Species Meet*. University of Minnesota Press.

Ireland, W.W. (1877) *On Idiocy and Imbecility*. London: J.A. Churchill.

Jarrett, S. and Tilley, E. (2022) 'The History of the History of Learning Disability', *British Journal of Learning Disabilities*, 50(2), pp. 132–142. Available at: https://doi.org/10.1111/bld.12461.

Jaworska, A. (2010) 'Caring and Full Moral Standing Redux', in E.F. Kittay and L. Carlson (eds) *Cognitive Disability and Its Challenge to Moral Philosophy*. Wiley-Blackwell, pp. 369–392.

Katz, I. (1991) 'Gordon Allport's "the Nature of Prejudice"', *Political Psychology*, 12(1), pp. 125–157.

Khaneman, D. (2011) *Thinking, Fast and Slow*. London: Penguin Books.

Kittay, E.F. and Carlson, L. (2010) *Cognitive Disability and Its Challenge to Moral Philosophy*. Chichester: Wiley-Blackwell.

Lathrop, E. (2020) 'Learning Difficulties: The Idiot and the Outsider in the Renaissance', in S. Anderson and L. Haydon (eds) *A Cultural History of Disability in the Renaissance*. London: Bloomsbury Publishing, pp. 133–150.

Linett, M. (2023) 'Mind the Gap', *Journal of Literary & Cultural Disability Studies*, 17(4), pp. 435–451. Available at: https://doi.org/10.3828/jlcds.2023.33.

Magnússon, S.G. (2021) 'One Story, One Person: The Importance of Micro/Bio Research for Disability Studies', in H.B. Sigurjónsdóttir and J.G. Rice (eds) *Understanding Disability Throughout History: Interdisciplinary Perspectives in Iceland from Settlement to 1936*. 1st edn. London: Routledge, pp. 46–57. Available at: https://doi.org/10.4324/9781003180180.

Matsumoto, D. (2013) 'Culture and Emotional Expression', *Understanding Culture*, pp. 271–287.

Mercier, H. and Sperber, D. (2018) *The Enigma of Reason: A New Theory of Human Understanding*. Great Britain: Penguin Books.

Mitchell, D.T. and Snyder, S.L. (2015) *The Biopolitics of Disability: Neoliberalism, Ablenationalism, and Peripheral Embodiment*. Ann Arbor: The University of Michigan Press.

Ojrzyńska, K. (2023) 'Ecorelational Aesthetics', *Journal of Literary & Cultural Disability Studies*, 17(4), pp. 489–505. Available at: https://doi.org/10.3828/jlcds.2023.36.

Shek-Noble, L. and Jones, C.T. (2023) 'Rethinking the Species Divide', *Journal of Literary & Cultural Disability Studies*, 17(4), pp. 407–414. Available at: https://doi.org/10.3828/jlcds.2023.31.

Stanovich, K.E. (1993) 'Dysrationalia: A New Specific Learning Disability', *Journal of Learning Disabilities*, 26(8), pp. 501–515. Available at: https://doi.org/10.1177/002221949302600803.

Stanovich, K.E., West, R.F. and Toplak, M.E. (2011) 'Intelligence and Rationality', in *The Cambridge Handbook of Intelligence*. New York: Cambridge University Press (Cambridge Handbooks in Psychology), pp. 784–826. Available at: https://doi.org/10.1017/CBO9780511977244.040.

Stefánsdóttir, G.V. and Ólafsdóttir, S. (2021) 'The Peculiar Attitude of the People: The Life and Social Conditions of One "Feeble-minded" Girl in the Early 20th Century', in H.B. Sigurjónsdóttir and J.G. Rice (eds) *Understanding Disability Throughout History: Interdisciplinary Perspectives in Iceland from Settlement to 1936*. 1st edn. London: Routledge, pp. 58–75. Available at: https://doi.org/10.4324/9781003180180.

Stefánsdóttir, G.V., Ólafsdóttir, S. and Magnússon, S.G. (2025) *Disability Studies Meets Microhistory: The Secret Life of Bíbí in Berlin*. Abingdon, Oxon: Routledge.

Swain, J. and French, S. (2008) *Disability on Equal Terms*. London: Sage.

Van Kleef, G.A. *et al.* (2016) 'Editorial: The Social Nature of Emotions', *Frontiers in Psychology*, 7. Available at: https://doi.org/10.3389/fpsyg.2016.00896.

Wong, A. (2020) *Disabled Oracles and the Coronavirus*. Disability Visibility Project. Available at: https://disabilityvisibilityproject.com/2020/03/18/coronavirus/ (Accessed: 25 June 2024).

6 Conclusion

I started this book by describing it as an attempt to learn *with* learning disability, rather than from or about learning disability. I conclude by returning to this idea; the idea that learning *with* is a means of striving to avoid objectification; a means of what Tim Ingold calls "togethering" rather than othering. Throughout the book, I have attempted to attend to – literally reach towards – learning disability, and to co-respond with learning disability: to be reflexive in considering and exploring learning disability. Although this exploration has been framed by the recent history of learning disability, it has also been an investigation into what learning disability can tell us about being human. And so the time has come to address the questions: What kind of thing is learning disability, and what can it tell us about being human?

My answer is that as an organising concept, learning disability affords an excellent opportunity to explore what it means to be human, precisely because so far in recent history, in Westernised cultures at least, people with learning disabilities have often been characterised as not fully human. Over the last two centuries, we have seen learning disability appear as various kinds of thing: as an object of curiosity, of scientific inquiry, of pity and charity, of existential terror and of control through abandonment. Whilst these discursive shifts have had profound impacts on the lives, and kinds of lives, people with learning disabilities lead, they have nevertheless been in one important sense superficial. Although our conceptualisations of, and regard for, people with learning disabilities may appear to shift over the course of decades, their status as an outgroup – perhaps still the ultimate outgroup – has hitherto largely remained unquestioned. The contours of our regard for people with learning disabilities have not changed much. To return to an ecological metaphor, the river might have meandered on its course over time, but the underlying rock has not moved. What this history shows us is that whilst we might like to think we are progressive and have become more inclusive, we have yet to eliminate our dehumanising core.

DOI: 10.4324/9781003411925-6

And yet it is not as simple as saying that everything to do with our thinking about learning disability is bad and wrong. Learning disability is useful trouble, it is a real problem, *because* it has much to teach us about what it means to be human. As an organising concept, learning disability helps demarcate the limits of and paradoxes our thinking about intelligence and personhood. On the one hand, the Humanist notion of intelligence marks those with intellectual impairments as an outgroup, and culture and discourse work hard to maintain this status. On the other hand, the Humanist notion of intelligence rests on a deeply flawed assumption of, and indeed worship of, individualist rationalist thought. It turns out the individualist, independent rational thinker is an ableist ideal nobody can really ever live up to.

Paradoxically, people with learning disabilities, rather than people of culture, appear to hold the key to understanding what it means to be human. This understanding goes beyond saying that people with learning disabilities afford non-disabled people noble opportunities to protect the vulnerable, or to demonstrate compassion. It goes beyond simply asserting that the two concepts – *learning disability* and *human* – need each other to make sense, or saying that they mirror each other. This understanding shows us how profoundly interdependent and intertwined learning-disabled and non-disabled people are. As Charles Darwin's great affection for his learning-disabled son Charles Waring shows, people can and do love the very people the dominant discourse – a discourse we may ourselves have helped to build – tells us we should reject, ostracise and eliminate. We care about them.

The current grand narrative of global crisis and contemporary theoretical intervention of posthumanism offer us the chance to think affirmatively about "what we are ceasing to be and what we might become" (Braidotti, 2019: 64). Some scholars of learning disability are already doing so in imaginative, provocative ways. For example, a recent doctoral study by Mark Bygroves into professional care practices enacted *with* – not just *on* or *for* – people labelled with Profound and Multiple Learning Disabilities revealed how care workers could establish authentic, deep, reciprocal relationships with the people they are caring for by embracing rather than fearing their own vulnerability (Bygroves, 2024). Vulnerability in this sense means being open to, and accepting of, ambiguity and uncertainty rather than trying to control every situation, encounter and activity. It means people nominated as "carers" *going along together with* people who are "cared-for" on a shared journey. Vulnerability conceptualised in this way thus catalyses deep and rich, tangled connections between learning-disabled and non-disabled people. Connections which are not merely transactional – one person caring for another, as a job – but are deeply ethical, sometimes even spiritual, and reveal our common humanity. This is a radically different notion of care to that which led to the establishment of asylums, long-stay hospitals, care in the community and the litany of abuses and scandals we have borne witness to. It is a radically different notion of vulnerability, since it not about one group perceiving another as vulnerable and then seeking to protect/control them. It is a conceptualisation of humanity where everyone has equally imperfect status and everyone is recognised as having their valuable gifts to give.

There are also promising developments in Ireland. A succession of National Access Plans over the past 30 years have sought to ensure equality of access to higher education as a fundamental principle of national educational policy. The current National Access Plan (Department of Further and Higher Education, Research, Innovation and Science and Higher Education Authority, 2022) specifically identifies students with intellectual disabilities (the preferred term in Ireland) as one of three main underrepresented groups – along with people who are socio-economically disadvantaged, and the Irish Traveller and Roma communities – for whom access must be improved. It is easy to be cynical about this: many governments and many institutions have talked the talk of inclusion (who, pre-Trump at least, would not claim to be inclusive these days?) without implementing the kinds of fundamental changes to structures, systems, processes and practices that genuine inclusion necessitates. So far, the rhetoric of inclusion has only got a few disabled people – and very few people with learning disabilities – through the university doors. And when they do get in, they tend to find built, social and pedagogical environments which are poorly suited to their needs. What is remarkable is that the Irish Government has recognised the people with learning disabilities can and should have a place at university. As a result, it has made available significant sums of money, known as Path 4 funding, to support the implementation Inclusivity Goal of the National Action Plan: it is walking the walk and not just talking the talk. This ideological and financial support from Central Government means that Irish Higher Education Institutions (HEIs) can make a legitimate claim to be leading the way in developing and implementing truly inclusive practices in relation to learning disability.

Crucially, the Path 4 funding has enabled the creation of a network of HEIs who work together on the inclusion of people with learning disabilities. Collaboration, not competition, is the key. This INCLUDE-ID network consists of nine HEIs offering third-level courses specifically for students with learning disabilities. Many offer what is known as co-learning as part of their course. Co-learning is where students with learning disabilities take the same classes as students without, with differentiated teaching and assessments, and additional supports as required. With education often conceived of a microcosm of society as well as preparation for it, these courses – at their best – can reasonably be considered as models of social inclusion. The presence of students with learning disabilities in mainstream classrooms is having positive effects on both students and lecturers. For instance, the Trinity Centre for People with Intellectual Disabilities (TCPID) at Trinity College Dublin, where I work, offers a co-learning opportunity with the School of English as part of its Certificate in Arts, Science and Inclusive Applied Practice. Students who take this option study Irish Literature alongside undergraduates taking Bachelor's degrees in English. Preliminary evaluative data shows not only are students with learning disabilities being welcomed into the class, but are bringing insights that would otherwise be missed. For example, the group analyse the poetry of Eavan Boland, which often explores issues related to the oppression and exclusion of women in Irish society. This is a topic where students with learning disabilities can make contributions to the class in a unique way, because many of them have experienced oppression and exclusion themselves. Their perceptions and perspectives help to deepen everyone's appreciation not only of Boland's work but also of humanity, society and exclusion more broadly. And this is exactly the kind of foregrounding of minoritised knowledges Posthumanism argues for.

Moreover, students with learning disabilities are visible on the campus and actively participate in the life of the College: in the Students Union, in mainstream student clubs and societies, and so on. Trinity College Dublin recently renamed its main library the Eavan Boland Library; one student with a learning disability who had taken the co-learning module was asked to read Boland's poetry as part of the social media campaign the College ran to mark the occasion. Trinity College Dublin was founded in 1592, almost exactly 100 years after da Vinci drew Vitruvian Man, and it is steeped in privilege, patriarchy, elitism and tradition. If people with learning disabilities can genuinely belong in such a place, on equal terms with those around them, then there is hope that they can belong everywhere. It would be wrong to present Trinity College Dublin as some kind of utopia for people with learning disabilities – there are still many flaws and obstacles to full and equal participation – but it is fair to say that they, and Ireland, have set out on a path towards one and are committed to staying the course.

This sense – not just of rightness and belonging, but also of appreciation for the gifts people with learning disabilities bring – extends beyond the College. Another key component of the ASIAP course for students with learning disabilities is internships and work placements. These are real, paid opportunities that most students take, and often turn into permanent jobs. TCPID partners with over 50 businesses for these placements, many of which are household names. Whilst we need to be cautious of reinscribing the neoliberal narrative that the only worthwhile life is one that makes an economic contribution, there is no doubt that these opportunities are highly valued by the students and the employers. Importantly, as with the co-learning, when students take these opportunities they are having positive effects on the organisations they go into, which are not merely tokenistic or feelgood corporate PR. At a recent event for TCPID business partners David McRedmond, the CEO of An Post, the Irish postal service, said that students with learning disabilities had "*had a humanising impact*" on the organisational culture, through things like enabling other staff to talk more openly about disability and disabled family members. Here we come back to where we started: same same but different. I suggested in Chapter 1 that although I am not disabled, I have significant relationships with disability and disabled people, which may be unique to me, but are probably not that much different to anybody else's. McRemond's remark appears to bear this claim out. It is also notable that McRedmond says that the hitherto dehumanised outgroup of people with learning disability are the ones having a humanising effect, once again suggesting that they hold the key to our understanding of what it means to be human. His claim again underscores our interdependence and the need to engage in continual meaningful dialogue with learning disability. By co-responding with learning disability, by learning *with* learning disability, we can all learn how to go along better together. And the world needs that right now.

References

Braidotti, R. (2019) *Posthuman Knowledge*. Cambridge: Polity Press.

Bygroves, M. (2024) *Disability Studies, Buber and Professional Practice: An Exploration into the Relationships Between Practitioners and People Described as Having Complex Needs*. EdD. Liverpool Hope University. Available at: https://hira.hope.ac.uk/id/eprint/4537/.

Department of Further and Higher Education, Research, Innovation and Science and Higher Education Authority (2022) *National Access Plan: A Strategic Action Plan for Equity of Access, Participation and Success in Higher Education 2022–2028*. Dublin: Government of Ireland. Available at: https://hea.ie/assets/uploads/2024/07/National-Access-Plan-2022-2028-FINAL.pdf (Accessed: 14 March 2025).

Index

Note: *Italic* page references indicate figures.

FSC
www.fsc.org
MIX
Papier | Fördert gute Waldnutzung
FSC® C083411

Kolibri 360 GmbH
Ferdinand-Jühlke-Straße 7
99095 Erfurt, Deutschland
produktsicherheit@kolibri360.de